James M. Peebles

**Lyceum Guide**

a collection of songs, hymns, and chants - lessons, readings, and recitations -

marches and calisthentics

James M. Peebles

**Lyceum Guide**

*a collection of songs, hymns, and chants - lessons, readings, and recitations - marches and calisthentics*

ISBN/EAN: 9783337265946

Printed in Europe, USA, Canada, Australia, Japan

Cover: Foto ©Lupo / pixelio.de

More available books at **www.hansebooks.com**

# THE LYCEUM GUIDE:

A COLLECTION OF

## SONGS, HYMNS, AND CHANTS;

Lessons, Readings, and Recitations;

### MARCHES AND CALISTHENICS.

(WITH ILLUSTRATIONS.)

TOGETHER WITH

### PROGRAMMES AND EXERCISES FOR SPECIAL OCCASIONS.

THE WHOLE DESIGNED

FOR THE USE OF PROGRESSIVE SUNDAY LYCEUMS.

BY

J. M. PEEBLES, J. O. BARRETT, AND EMMA TUTTLE.

THE MUSICAL DEPARTMENT BY JAMES G. CLARK.

"HUMAN NATURE IS DIVINE."

BOSTON:
PUBLISHED BY ADAMS AND COMPANY,
25 BROMFIELD STREET.
LONDON: J. BURNS, 15 SOUTHAMPTON ROW.
1870.

C. J. PETERS & SON, STEREOTYPERS, BOSTON, MASS.

# PREFACE.

In issuing THE LYCEUM GUIDE, we have no other apology to make, than that we have, as practical workers in the Lyceum, felt its need. The numerous responses to our published card, from conductors and others interested in this movement, assure us that this want is generally experienced.

In the working of a Lyceum, a book is demanded containing plain directions for its establishment, its calisthenics and marching, music, lessons, and recitations, and yet of moderate size, and cheap enough to be within the reach of every child as well as adult member. It has been our aim to produce such a book; so plain in all its directions, that, wherever a Lyceum is desired, it will furnish all required information; and those who are to act as officers can, by its assistance, go forward without the expense attending the procuring of an individual already versed in the methods of organization. The size of the GUIDE gives small indication of the labor expended on its pages. The editor of our Musical Department is the prince of ballad-singers, and has a national fame as author of some of the best sacred, patriotic, and pathetic songs in our language. Many of his finest compositions appear in our work, never before having been published except in sheet form.

The exercises for reading have been constructed with strict reference to presenting the best expressions of truth, moral purity, and nobility of life.

We have also endeavored to make our work cosmopolitan. Spiritualism is finding its way to all countries and all peoples. Its enduring base is the coming generations, and the Lyceum is the foundation on which the perpetuity of its sublime philosophy rests. As it belongs to mankind, it should not be narrowed to a nation, nor be marshalled under national ensigns, but its banners should be stamped only with colors emblematic of the broadest and most catholic truth. Although we, as Americans, are proud of our beautiful national banner, and cherish sacredly the sentiment of patriotism, we respect the sentiment as well in the bosom of an Englishman, a German, or a Frenchman.

We wish to express our thanks to the friends who have aided us in words and works, and especially to acknowledge our indebtedness to Joseph John, Professor in the Academy of Fine Arts in Philadelphia, for his scientific and admirable arrangement of the COLOR DEPARTMENT.

Also to the many noble workers who are not represented on our pages, for want of space, but whose energetic labors have inspired us constantly in the doing of a responsible but pleasant duty.

We have made the book which we offer you as complete as possible at present, but we do not assume that it is a finality. As the years go by, and our cause advances, the requirements of the day may change, and our task be superseded. If it be by something better, we shall be glad to greet the advance.

BOSTON, Sept. 1, 1870.      THE EDITORS.

## CHERISH KINDLY FEELINGS.

Words by Mrs. M. A. Kidder.  Music by J. G. C.

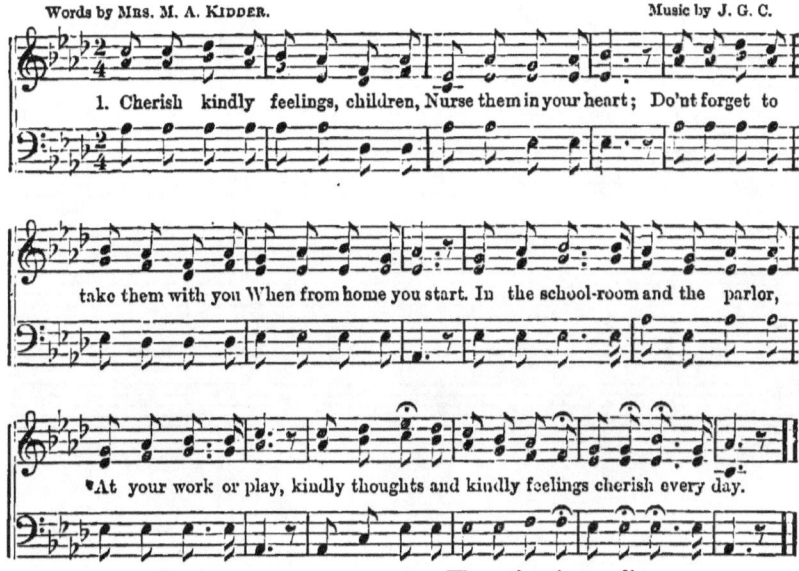

1. Cherish kindly feelings, children, Nurse them in your heart; Do'nt forget to take them with you When from home you start. In the school-room and the parlor, At your work or play, kindly thoughts and kindly feelings cherish every day.

2
Cherish kindly feelings, children,
  Toward the old and poor,
For you know they've many blighting
  Hardships to endure;
Try to make their burdens lighter,
  Help them in their need,
By some sweet and kindly feeling,
  Or some generous deed.

3
Cherish kindly feelings, children,
  While on earth you stay,
They will scatter light and sunshine
  All along your way;
Make the path of duty brighter,
  Make your trials less,
And whate'er your lot or station,
  Bring you happiness.

### The Art of Beauty.

1
Would you have a form of beauty?
  Then be good and true,
Doing every little duty
  Which belongs to you.
Cherish virtues, bright and golden,
  Weave them in your lives;
'Tis a motto true and olden,
  "Grace on goodness thrives."

2
Do you wish for noble features?
  Cultivate the mind,
Harbor no disturbing passions,
  Singly, or combined.
Leave strong drink, that mischief breeder,
  Utterly alone;
Beauty is not flaming poppies
  On the visage sown.

3
Would you have a fine complexion?
  Do not keep late hours;
Night is resting-time, my children,
  Sleep, like lily flowers.
In the daytime you may wander
  Where the sweet pure air
Bathes the meadows, hills, and woodlands,
  Growing fresh and fair.

4
Do you long for cheeks like roses?
  In the morning dew
Go and ask the pink carnations
  Where they get their hue.
Train the honeysuckle blossoms
  Which the wild bee sips,
And its rich and glowing colors
  Will repaint your lips.

2.

Let us love while we live, and our memory will rise
Like a halo of light from the grave,
As the day from the deep, lends a glow to the eyes,
That are guarding the gloom of the wave.
There's a life in the soul that is better by far,
Than the glitter of glory or gold, —
It may fade in the noon, but will shine like a star
When the proud world is darksome and cold.

## AN OPENING SONG.

AIR.—"*Crystal Fountain.*"

Words by EMMA TUTTLE.  Music by H. M. HIGGINS.

1. Oh, ye who once were mortals, Enrobed, like us in clay, Come down from heaven's blue meadows, And be with us to-day.— Instruct us, loving angels, The way your glory came, And wreathe about our foreheads Truth's glowing ring of flame.

2
Bring down a breath from Eden,
 And let us breathe it in,
Till its surpassing sweetness
 Makes us forget to sin!
Our hearts are reaching upward,
 Like singing larks in spring,
And every soul is willing
 To learn the truths you bring.

3
Come down, oh, blessed angels,
 Make earth and heaven one,
And when our paths are shadowed,
 Be ye our rising sun;
Unfold us in God's wisdom,
 His beauty and his love—
And may the earth-life fit us
 To be like you above.

## Closing Song.

AIR.—"*Crystal Fountain.*"

1
Our hearts are bound together,
  A chain of chaliced blooms,
Wooing the dews of heaven,
  And rich in sweet perfumes.
The skill of angel fingers
  Combined the circlet fair,
And bade us be love's lilies,
  The dusky earth shall wear.

2
We love our march and music,
  Our banners bright unfurled,
Our lessons and our teachers,
  And all the great wide world.
Our souls behold God's goodness
  And blossom into prayer,—
Prayer which shall speak in actions
  Of kindness everywhere.

3
We met with glances sparkling
  To touch the skirts of Truth,
And plant the germs of wisdom
  Along the banks of youth.
The brightly tinted roses,
  Will bless us bye and bye,
And our glad souls will wear them
  Through death in victory.

4
We part, and may each member,
  Wherever he may go,
Work for the poor and sinful,
  But keep as pure as snow!
Our confidence is boundless,
  For though we walk with men,
Angels will watch and guide us
  Until we meet again.

*Emma Tuttle.*

---

## Keep A Pure Heart.

AIR.—"*Crystal Fountain.*"

1
Come let us sing together,
  As leaves sing on a tree,
When through the swaying branches
  The wind pipes merrily.
Let us repeat a lesson
  Our Angel guides impart;
That he shall be most blessed
  Who keeps the purest heart.

2.
We learn a loving spirit
  Will beautify the face,
And fashion every feature
  To soft angelic grace.
While sinful thoughts, and feelings
  Will spoil the brightest eyes,
And mar the lips of childhood,
  Though steeped in rosy dyes.

3.
Each child may make his spirit
  An angel, clad in clay,
And do an angel's mission
  To others every day.
How many bleeding gashes
  His little hands may bind;
How sweet the ways of Heaven
  Thus placed before mankind!

4
Oh, who would covet brilliants
  To glitter on his brow?
Or who win empty honors
  That all the world may bow?
Since well we know the lesson
  Our angel guides impart;
That he shall be most blessed
  Who keeps the purest heart.

5
Then let us join together,
  And try with all our might,
Amid' Earth's dust and tumult,
  To keep our mantles white;
To think and do no evil,
  To hurl no venomed dart,
For he shall be most blessed,
  Who keeps the purest heart.

*Emma Tuttle.*

# THE TURF SHALL BE MY FRAGRANT SHRINE.

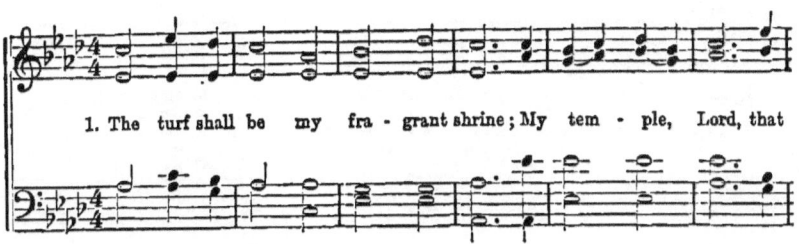

1. The turf shall be my fra-grant shrine; My tem-ple, Lord, that

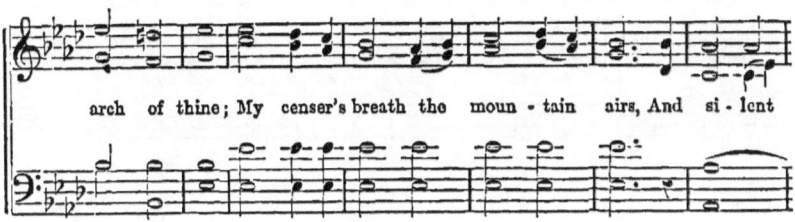

arch of thine; My censer's breath the moun-tain airs, And si-lent

thoughts my on-ly prayers, And si-lent thoughts my on-ly prayers.

2
My choir shall be the moonlit waves,
When murm'ring homeward to their caves,
Or when the stillness of the sea,
E'en more than music breathes of thee!

3
I'll seek some glade with beauty fraught,
All light and silent, like thy thought;
And the pale stars shall be at night
The only eyes that watch my rite.

4
Thy heaven, on which 'tis bliss to look,
Shall be my pure and shining book,
Where I shall read, in words of flame,
The glories of thy wondrous name.

5
There's nothing bright, above, below,
From flowers that bloom to stars that glow,
But in its light my soul can see
Some feature of thy Deity.

## CHRISTMAS BELLS. Concluded.

## MORN AMID THE MOUNTAINS.

2
Hymns of praise are ringing
Through the leafy wood;
Songsters, sweetly singing,
Warble, "God is good."
Warble, etc.

3
Now the glad sun, breaking,
Pours a golden flood;

Deepest vales, awaking,
Echo, "God is good."
Echo, etc.

4
Wake, and join the chorus,
Child with soul endued;
God, whose smile is o'er us,
Evermore is good.
Ever, etc.

## O HEAR THE SHOUT OF THE BRAVE RING OUT. 29
[Concluded.]

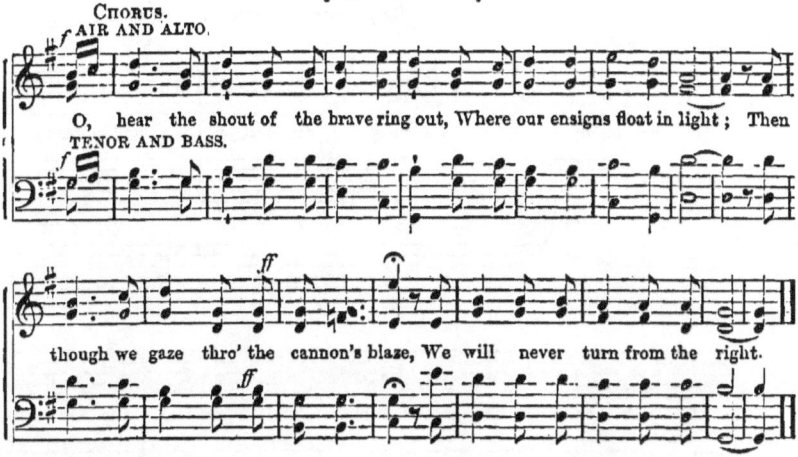

O, hear the shout of the brave ring out, Where our ensigns float in light; Then though we gaze thro' the cannon's blaze, We will never turn from the right.

## THE POWER OF LITTLE THINGS.

1. A trav-'ler on the road Strewed a-corns on the lea, And one took root and sprout-ed up, And grew in-to a tree.

2
A spring had lost its way
  Amid the grass and fern ;
A passing stranger scooped a well,
  Where weary men might turn.

3
Years passed, and lo! the well,
  By summer never dried,
Had cooled ten thousand parching tongues,
  And saved a life beside.

4
A man amid a crowd
  That thronged the daily mart,
Let fall a word of hope and love
  Unstudied from the heart.

5
O germ! O fount! O love!
  O thought at random cast!
Ye were but little at the first,
  But mighty at the last.

# MARCHING SONG.

MELODY.—"*Old Mountain Tree.*" By permission of OLIVER DITSON & Co.

Words by EMMA TUTTLE. Music by J. G. CLARK.

MARCHING SONG. Concluded. 31

2
We are marching on, we are marching on,
  And our feet grow sure each day,
We can catch a breath from the landscapes
  To which we march away.    [bright
There are voices ringing back to us,
  All glad with their cheerings sweet,
And who would fear, when we almost hear
  The chime of the angels' feet?

3
We are marching on, we are marching on,
  But not in idleness;
This world of ours is a place to learn,
  To toil, to love, to bless.

So day by day we must grow in soul;
  In wisdom, strength, and truth,
As we march along to our cheery song,
  Through the pleasant paths of youth.

4
We are marching on, we are marching on,
  To the fair lands bathed in light,
Where wisdom rules in majesty,
  And Heaven is doing right.
We ask no pledge that a crown of gems
  Upon our brows shall glow,
For the silver flowers of immortal bowers,
  Within each heart will grow.

## SPEAK! NO MATTER WHAT BETIDE.

*Earnestly.*  GEORGE F. ROOT.

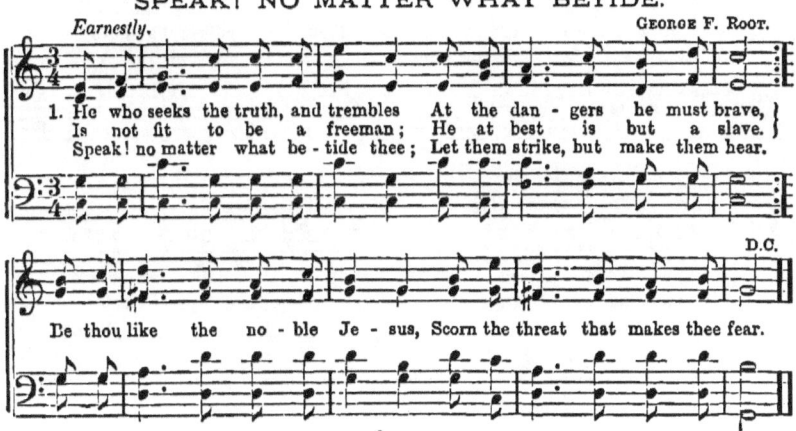

1. He who seeks the truth, and trembles  At the dan-gers he must brave,
   Is not fit to be a freeman;  He at best is but a slave.
   Speak! no matter what be-tide thee;  Let them strike, but make them hear.

Be thou like the no-ble Je-sus, Scorn the threat that makes thee fear.

2
Be thou like the first apostles;
  Never fear, thou shalt not fall;
If a free thought seeks expression,
  Speak it boldly! speak it all!
Face thine enemies, accusers;
  Scorn the prison, rack, or rod!
And if thou hast truth to utter,
  Speak, and leave the rest with God!

## A REQUIEM.

Words by EMMA TUTTLE.   Melody by JAMES G. CLARK.   Arranged by Dr. E. L. PERRY.

1. Low mur-murs of mu-sic, march slow on our hearts, For O! they are pierced by death's cru-el-est darts, We saw a dear com-rade turn off from the way, And van-ish in shadows se-pul-chral and gray, The curtains have dropped o'er the beau-ti-ful eyes, And vainly we question the lips for re-plies, But soft-ly a cho-rus floats down from the spheres With

2. Wail, wail o'er the per-ish-ing dir-ges of woe! Bind wreaths of white flowers on the forehead of snow, Lament for the days which too quick-ly went by, As rose-clouds of morning fade out in the sky, And treasure all mem-o-ries ten-der and pure, While friendship and hearts which can love shall en-dure; But list to the cho-rus which floats from the spheres, With

## A REQUIEM. Concluded.

3

The grave seemeth cold, and its silence too hushed,
For one who so late in life's rosy tints blushed;
The body we place pain in the darkness so deep,
But know the dear soul has not fallen asleep.
Ah! blessèd the gospel which scatters its balm,
To hearts which are singing death's low minor psalm;
And blessed the chorus which breaks on our ears,
So hopeful and glad from the bright angel spheres.

# THE LYCEUM MARCH.

# THE LYCEUM MARCH. Concluded.

# WHERE HAVE THE BEAUTIFUL GONE?

# THE WORLD IS GROWING GOOD.

MELODY. — "*Gentle May.*" By permission of ROOT & CADY.

Words by EMMA TUTTLE.  Music by JAMES G. CLARK.

## THE WORLD IS GROWING GOOD. Concluded.

Chorus.

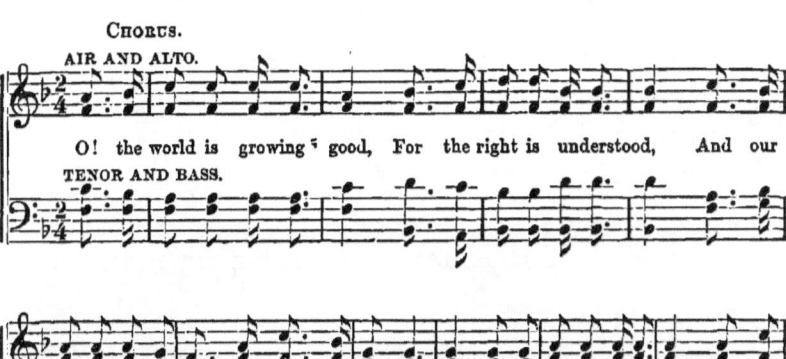

2
Wrong is fleeing Earth's high places,
And we'll shout for honest faces,
And for hearts as strong as time, and true as steel.
She is loosing all her leases,
And her systems fall to pieces,
While we cheer for men who reason, learn, and feel.

Chorus.

O, the world is growing good,
For the right is understood,
And our little lives are full of brilliant chances.
Martyrs have not died in vain,
And we chant a glad refrain
As we follow Truth wherever she advances!

3.
O, a thousand lights are streaming,
Brighter far than poet's dreaming,
Through the darkness which has shut away the skies.
Lo, we see illumined faces
Lighting up the ether spaces,
And we meet the earnest gaze of angel eyes.
Chorus.— O, the world, &c.

4
Then we'll raise a ringing chorus,
For the golden days before us,
While we work to bring them nearer, day by day,
Heaven is not so far above us,
That its inmates cannot love us,
And lean out to hear us singing on our way.
Chorus. — O! the world, &c.

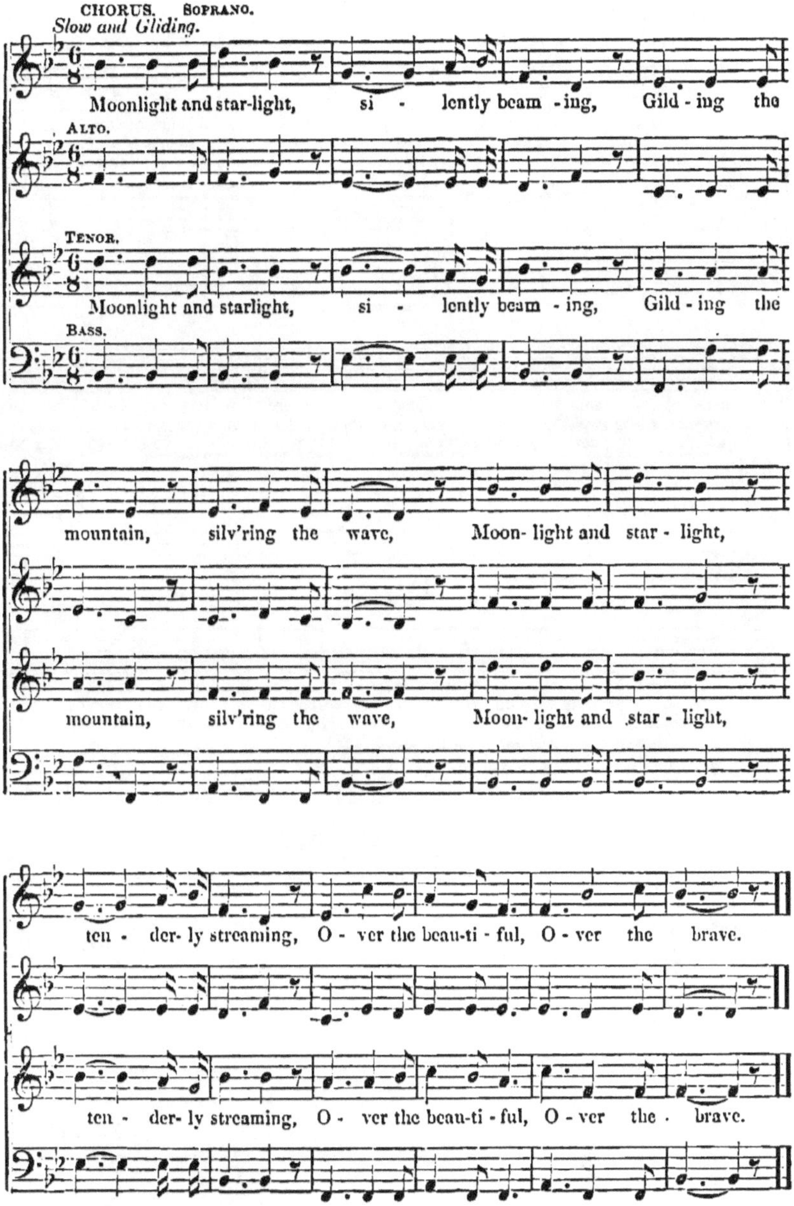

# MOONLIGHT AND STARLIGHT. Concluded.

**CHORUS. SOPRANO.**
*Slow and Gliding.*

Moonlight and star-light, si - lently beam - ing, Gild - ing the mountain, silv'ring the wave, Moon- light and star - light, ten - der- ly streaming, O - ver the beau-ti - ful, O - ver the brave.

## WE SHALL MEET OUR FRIENDS IN THE MORNING.

MELODY. — "*When You and I were Soldier Boys.*" By permission of OLIVER DITSON & Co.

Words by EMMA TUTTLE. Music by J. G. CLARK.

1. O, the cheering dreams we know, As we toil a-long be-low, To the country where we all shall rest together, friends,......... Where the sum-mer al-ways stays With her blossom brightened days, And we need not face earth's storm-y, win-try weather, friends.

2. Oft our hearts grow sick with pain, And we hope and pray in vain That our Father make more sweet earth's bit-ter fountains, friends,......... Then we wipe away our tears, And look past these cloudy years, Where a ro-sy dawn lights up Heaven's ver-nal mountains, friends.

3. We shall scarce remem-ber there, All these bat-tle scars we bear. How we cleft a path to glo-ry Through the shadows, friends,......... For our tri-umph will be sweet, And most ju-bi-lant our feet, When we tread, at last, God's great star-gleam-ing meadows, friends.

# WE SHALL MEET OUR FRIENDS IN THE MORNING
## [Concluded.]

## ARE WE NOT BROTHERS?

From "*The Spiritual Harp.*"

1. Hushed be the bat-tle's fearful roar, The warrior's rushing call! Why should the earth be drenched with gore? Are we not broth-ers all? Are we not brothers all?

2
Want, from the starving poor depart!
Chains, from the captive fall!
Great God, subdue th' oppressor's heart!
Are we not brothers all?

3
Sect, clan, and nation, oh, strike down
Each mean partition-wall!

Let love the voice of discord drown, —
Are we not brothers all?

Let love and truth and peace alone
Hold human hearts in thrall,
That heaven its work at length may own,
And men be brothers all.

## THE OLD AND THE NEW.

Words by J. G. WHITTIER.  From "*The Spiritual Harp.*"

1. Oh! sometimes gleams upon our sight, Through present wrong, th' eternal right! And step by step, since time began, We see the steady gain of man. That all of good the past has had Remains to make our own time glad, Our common dai-ly life divine, And eve-ry land a Pal-es-tine.

2
We lack but open eye and ear
To find the Orient's marvels here,
The still, small voice in autumn's hush,
Yon maple wood the burning bush.
For still the New transcends the Old,
In signs and tokens manifold;
Slaves rise up men; the olive waves
With roots deep set in battle graves.

3
Through the harsh noises of the day
A low, sweet prelude finds its way;
Through clouds of doubt and creeds of fear
A light is breaking calm and clear.
Henceforth my heart shall sigh no more
For olden time and holier shore;
God's love and blessing, then and there,
Are now and here and everywhere.

# THE GOLDEN SIDE.

From "*The Spiritual Harp.*"
Words by Mrs. M. A. Kidder.  Music by S. W. Tucker.

1. There is man-y a rest in the road of life, If we on-ly would stop to take it, And man-y a tone from the bet-ter land, If the queru-lous heart would make it! To the sunny soul, that is full of hope, And whose beauti-ful trust ne'er fall-eth, The grass is green and the flow'rs are bright, Though the wint-ry storm prevail-eth.

2
Better hope, though the clouds o'er you hang
 Ever keep the sad eyes still lifted ; [so low;
The sweet sunny sky will be peeping through
 When the ominous clouds are rifted!
There was ne'er a night but that had a day,
 Or an evening without a morning ;
The darkest hour, as the proverb goes,
 Is the hour before the dawning.

3
There is many a gem in the path of life,
 Which we pass in our idle pleasure,
That's richer by far than the jewelled crown,
 Or the miserly hoarded treasure ;

It may be the love of a little child,
 Or a dear mother's prayers to heaven,
Or some lone wanderer's grateful thanks
 For a cup of water given.

4
Oh, 'tis better to weave in the web of life
 The most beautiful golden filling,
To do all life's work with a cheerful heart,
 And with hands that are swift and willing,
Than to snap the frail, tender, minute threads
 Of our curious lives asunder ;
And then blame heaven for the tangled ends,
 And still sit and grieve and wonder.

## REST FOR THE WEARY.

2
They are fitting up our mansions,
Which eternally shall stand,
For our stay will not be transient
In that happy spirit land.

CHORUS. — There is rest, &c.

3
Death itself shall then be vanquished,
And its sting shall be withdrawn;
Shout for gladness, O ye mortals,
Hail with joy the rising morn.

CHORUS. — There is rest, &c.

## HARD TIMES COME AGAIN NO MORE.

By permission of OLIVER DITSON & Co.  Music by S. C. FOSTER.

# LET US GATHER UP THE SUNBEAMS.

Arranged from HANDEL.

## LET US GATHER UP THE SUNBEAMS. Concluded. 61

2.
If we knew the baby fingers
 Pressed against the window pane,
 Would be cold, and stiff to-morrow —
 Never trouble us again —
 Would the bright eyes of our darling
 Catch the frown upon our brow;
 Would the print of rosy fingers
 Vex us then as they do now?

3
Ah, these little ice-cold fingers,
 How they point our memories back
 To the hasty word and action
 Strewn along our backward track!

How these little hands remind us,
 As in snowy grace they lie,
 Not to scatter thorns — but roses —
 For our reaping by and by.

4
Let us gather up the sunbeams
 Lying all around our path;
 Let us keep the wheat and roses,
 Casting out the thorns and chaff;
 Let us find our sweetest comfort
 In the blessings of to-day,
 With a patient hand removing
 All the briers from our way.

## WORK IS PRAYER.

From "*The Psalms of Life.*"

Words by DUGANNE.     Music by ANSORGE.

1. Brothers! be ye who ye may — Sons of men! I bid ye pray! Pray unceasing — pray with might! Pray in darkness — pray in light! — Life hath yet no hours to spare — Life is toil — and toil is prayer.

2
Life is toil, and all that lives,
 Sacrifice of labor gives!
 Water, fire, and air, and earth,
 Rest not, pause not, from their birth —
 Sacred toil doth nature share —
 Love and labor! — work is prayer!

3
Patriot! toiling for thy kind!
 Thou shalt break the chains that bind! —
 Shape thy thought, and mold thy plan,

Toil for freedom — toil for man!
 Sagely think, and boldly dare —
 Labor! labor! — work is prayer!

4
Brother! — round thee brothers stand —
 Pledge thy truth, and give thy hand —
 Raise the downcast — help the weak,
 Toil for good — for virtue speak;
 Let thy brethren be thy care —
 Labor! labor! — work is prayer.

## WE LOVE THE FATHER.

[This little song was chanted by a happy group of children from the Summer-Land, and the lady medium who heard the sweet symphony was enabled to record both the words and the music.*] "Lyceum Manual."

1. We love the Father, He's so good, We see him in the flower, We hear him in the rain-drop, He speaketh in the shower, His smile is in the sun-light, His beauty in the bow, We hear his whisper in the breeze, And in the zephyr low.

2
His wisdom's in the dew-drop,
   That sparkles on the lea,
His truth is in the violet's hue,
   His love's in all we see.
He's merciful and kind to all,
   And ever just and true,
To those who truly on Him call,
   He ever gives their due.

3
He soothes the striken mourner's heart,
   He aids the weary soul,
And lends them, while he joy imparts,
   To an eternal goal,

In Nature's grandest works we find,
   His great immortal skill:
Then let us each with humble mind,
   Learn to obey his will.

4
Oh, may we ever gentle be,
   In all our works and ways,
In all our conduct frank and free,
   And his great goodness praise.
In everything we look upon,
   His image we can see.
We love the Father, He's so good,
   And teaches us to be.

\* With additional words by Miss E. C. ODIORNE.

# O SACRED PRESENCE.

### Chant.

1. O sacred presence! Life Divine! We rear for thee no gild-ed shrine!
2. We will not mock thy holy name, with titles high, of emp-ty fame,
3. All souls in circling orbits run, around thee as their cen-tral sun;

Unfashioned by the hand of art, Thy temple is the child-like heart;
For thou with all thy works and ways, Art far beyond our fee-ble praise;
And as the planets roll and burn, To thee, O Lord! for light we turn;

No tearful eye, no bended knee, No servile speech we bring to thee;
But freely as the birds that sing, The soul's spontaneous gift we bring,
Nor life, nor death, nor time, nor space, Shall rob us of our name or place;

For thy great love tunes ev'ry voice, And makes each trusting soul re-joice.
And like the fragrance of the flowers, We con-se-crate to thee our powers.
But we shall love thee and adore, Through end-less a-ges ev-er-more.

**Chorus.** *Lively.*

Then strike your lyres, ye angel choirs! The sound prolong, O white-robed throng! Till ev'ry creature joins the song.

## TRUTH. Chant.

1. O Truth, we turn to thee as to the | light. | Thou art a..Treasure above all | price.
2. To thee we bow the knee as to our | king. | Thou guidst in..pleasant | places ;
3. Lifting the dark clouds from our | souls. | Revealing the joys of | heaven.
4. Thy celestial beacon | gleams. | Over the shadows and..valley of | death.
5. Thou art the harmony of nature's | laws. | The goal of..Perfect | spirit.
6. Thou art the King of the | world, | our Redeemer..Saviour and | friend.
7. Our feet shall be swift at thy | bidding, | Our voices ever..ascend in thy | praise. A-men.

## WALK WITH THE BEAUTIFUL. Chant.

1
Walk with the beautiful and with the grand,
Let nothing on the earth thy | feet de- | ter ;
Sorrow may lead thee weeping by the hand,
But give not all thy bosom | thoughts to | her,
Walk | with the | beautiful.

2
I hear thee say, The beautiful ! what is it ?
O, thou art | darkly | ignorant! be sure
'Tis no long, weary road its form to visit,
For thou caus't make it smile be- | side thy
Then | love the | beautiful. [door

3
Ay, love it ; 'tis a sister that will bless,
And teach thee patience when the | heart is | lonely :
The angels love it, for they wear its dress,
And thou art made a little | lower | only,
Then | love the | beautiful.

## THE ANGELS OF CONSOLATION. Chant.

1. With silence only as their benediction, the | angels | come,
Where in the shadow of a great af- | flic...tion, the | soul sits | dumb.
2. Yet would we say, what every heart approveth, our | Father's | will.
Calling to him the dear ones whom he | lov..eth is | mercy | still.
3. Not upon us, or ours, the solemn angel hath | evil | wrought ;
The fun'ral anthem is a glad e- | van..gel ; the | good die | not!
4. God calls our loved ones, but we lose not wholly what | he has | given ;
They live on earth in thought and deed, as tru...ly as | in his | heaven.

## INVOCATION TO THE ANGELS.

### Chant.

### THE NIGHT HAS GATHERED UP HER MOONLIT FRINGES.

### Chant.

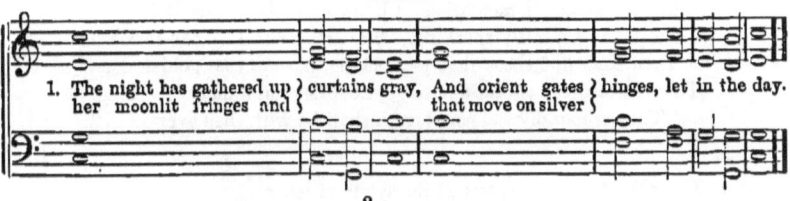

2

The morning sun his golden eyelash raises
    O'er | eastern | hills ;
The happy Summer-bird, with matin | praises,
    The | thicket | fills.

3

And nature's dress, with softly tinted roses,
    And | lilies | wrought,
Through all its varied unity discloses
    God's | perfect | thought.

4

Oh drop, my soul, the burden that oppresses,
    And | cares that | rule,
That I may prove the whispering wildernesses,
    | Heaven's | vesti- | bule!

5

For I can hear, despite material warden,
    And | earthly | locks,
A still small voice, and know that through his garden
    The | Father | walks.

# MUSICAL READINGS.*

### No. 1.

#### Always a Future.

1. I BEHELD a golden portal in the visions of my slumber,
    And through it streamed the radiance of a never-setting day,
   While angels tall and beautiful, and countless without number,
    Were giving gladsome greeting to all who came that way.
   And the gate, forever swinging, made no grating, no harsh ringing,
    Melodious as the singing of one that we adore;
   And I heard a chorus swelling, grand beyond a mortal's telling;
    And the burden of that chorus was Hope's glad word, "Evermore!"

✗

2. And, as I gazed and listened, came a mortal wildly weeping:
    "I have lost my hopes forever; one by one they went away:
   The idols of my patient love the cold grave hath in keeping;
    Life is one long lamentation; I know no night nor day!"
   Then the angel, softly speaking, "Stay, mourner, stay thy shrieking:
    Thou shalt find those thou art seeking, beyond that golden door."
   Then I heard the chorus swelling, grand beyond a mortal's telling,
    "They whom thy sad soul loveth shall be with thee evermore!"

✗

3. I saw the toiler enter, to rest for aye from labor;
    The weary-hearted exile there found his native land;
   The beggar there could greet the king as equal and as neighbor;
    The crown had left the kingly brow, the staff the beggar's hand.
   And the gate, forever swinging, made no grating, no harsh ringing,
    Melodious as the singing of one that we adore;
   And the chorus still was swelling, grand beyond a mortal's telling,
    While the vision faded from me, with the glad word, "Evermore!"

* In these readings, singing may be introduced at the points marked with ✗.

### Rest for the Weary.

*Music on page 58.*

**1.**

In the angels' home in glory
 There remains a land of rest:
There the loved have gone before us,
 To fulfil their soul's request.

*Chorus.*— There is rest for the weary,
 There is rest for the weary,
 There is rest for the weary,
  There is rest for you.
 On the other side of Jordan,
 In the sweet fields of Eden,
 Where the tree of life is blooming,
  There is rest for you.

**2.**

They are fitting up our mansions,
 Which eternally shall stand;
For our stay will not be transient
 In that happy spirit-land.

*Chorus.*— There is rest, &c.

**3.**

Death itself shall then be vanquished,
 And its sting shall be withdrawn.
Shout for gladness, O ye mortals!
 Hail with joy the rising morn.

*Chorus.*— There is rest, &c.

---

## No. 2.

### The Angels.

THE angels stand by the pure in heart in their transfigured beauty, and surround them with a sphere of light and melody.

They come to lead the weary pilgrims from the rude scenes of life to mansions of inward rest.

Their presence is marked by an irridescent glory, and their footsteps are luminous long after they have passed.

They breathe a holy calm into the wounded heart.

The glory of their presence dissipates the darkness of the world; their smiles dissolve the frosts of years; they restore the springtime of the affections, and make life's barren wastes bloom like the gardens of Paradise.   *S. B. Brittan.*

### The Angel Era.

**1.**

Lo, in the golden sky
 We angel forms descry;
Celestial hosts descend to-day.
 The friends of early years,
 From their exalted spheres,
Walk with us on our earthly way.

**2.**

No more we sigh and mourn
 O'er loved and loving gone.
They throng around the path we go;
 They bless us in our home,
 Are with us where we roam,
Our conflicts and our triumphs know.

### 3.

The grave hath lost its dread:
To us there are no dead;
But all do live and love as one.
Our doubts and fears depart:
In each and every heart
The holy will of God is done.

### 4.

Thanks, grateful thanks, we raise
To Him who crowns our days
With blessings numberless and free:
In one united band,
As brothers, hand in hand,
Henceforth mankind in joy shall be.

*John S. Adams.*

## No. 3.

### The Beautiful.

BEAUTY is the robe of divinity itself, the privilege of angels. There is a spiritual beauty gleaming from the features of the good and pure, which transfigures them into a divine expression.

Beauty, called into being by the genial warmth of goodness, and inspired by the soft radiance of joy, expands into bloom only in the bland atmosphere of love.

Spiritual love gives grace to every movement, light to the eye, sweetness to the mouth, color to the cheek, and beautiful animation to the whole figure.

Absolute purity of heart and life is the richest human possession.

"Give ear," said the old Aryan of India, "to the instructions of prudence, and let the precepts of truth sink deep into your hearts, O my children! So shall the charms of your minds add lustre to the elegance of your forms; and your beauty, like the rose it resembles, shall retain its sweetness when the bloom is withered."

### Walk with the Beautiful.
*Chant on page 64.*

#### 1.
Walk with the beautiful and with the grand:
Let nothing on the earth thy feet deter.
Sorrow may lead thee weeping by the hand,
But give not all thy bosom thoughts to her.
    Walk with the beautiful.

#### 2.
I hear thee say, "The beautiful! what is it?"
Oh, thou art darkly ignorant! Be sure

'Tis no long, weary road its form to visit,
For thou canst make it smile beside thy door.
    Then love the beautiful.

#### 3.
Ay, love it: 'tis a sister that will bless,
And teach thee patience when the heart is lonely.
The angels love it, for they wear its dress;
And thou art made a little lower only.
    Then love the beautiful.

## No. 4.

### In Knowledge there is Safety.

WHO would tarry on the lowlands of ignorance? Are not the highlands of knowledge more broad, bright, and beautiful? Let us go up where the breezes are fresh from sunlit mountain-peaks, and light floods the landscapes.

There are no treacherous pitfalls, but we may see and know that our feet are sure. Wisdom smiles under her coronet of stars, and beckons our standard-bearers.

Lead us onward, O evangels of Truth!

There is no danger so appalling as that of ignorance. Groping in its darkness, we stumble upon all conceivable sorrows and follies.

The violation of the laws of physical existence fills countless graves with forms which the spirit should have worn much longer, for its highest good. In ignorance we unwittingly scar and stain our souls with sins which pain and weaken us here and in heaven.

Lead us onward, O divine wisdom!

Ignorance involves nations in war, and lays low their champions of honor, amidst the wailing of broken homes and hearts.

Who can count the multitudes which have perished by her dusky hand?

Lead us onward, O divine wisdom!

### The Song of Learning.

BY EMMA TUTTLE.

Tune,—"We shall meet our friends in the morning." Page 43.

1.

Blend your voices, full and strong,
In a grand redemption song,
And we'll sing the praise of noble, clear-browed learning.
How the night will fade away
In a bright and peaceful day
When we all can sing the pleasant song of learning!

*Chorus.*— Oh, rally at her call!
She has laurels for us all,
Which time cannot blight with decay.

We can wear them through the gate,
Where the tearful angels wait,
And point to the land far away.
Then join in the song of learning,
Then join in the song of learning,
Then join in the song of learning,
And march to the gates of day.

2.

Oh! the world has suffered long
'Neath the crushing heel of wrong,
While Ignorance blocked up the road to learning:
But her dusky form must fall;
For we rally, one and all,
Where the stars shine round the brow of noble Learning.

*Chorus.* — Oh, rally, &c.

3.
In the majesty of worth,
Angel forms will walk the earth,
When we all can sing the pleasant song of learning.

Whensoo'er a truth is said,
Woo its brightness to your head;
For the saviour of the world is noble Learning.
*Chorus.* — Oh, rally, &c.

## No. 5.

### Remember the Poor.

DO not call loudly upon God to remember the poor, when thou art constantly forgetting their needs and their sorrows.

Benevolent actions are the most holy prayers; and he who giveth to the needy enriches his own soul.

✕

Be just, as well as generous; be willing to remunerate labor honestly and fairly: then shall warm hearts know better days, sighing voices grow merry, and the old chains of want be broken.

✕

Riches often slip away as silently and as irrecoverably as the moments of life. They are evanescent and changeable; and only as far as they aid us in spiritual growth are they of lasting value.

"The poor man's lot to-day
May become our own to-morrow;"

and those who are now rejoicing in opulence wail the song of "Hard times, come again no more."

✕

### Hard Times, Come Again no More.

*Music on page 59.*

1.

Let us pause in life's pleasures, and count its many tears,
While we all sup sorrow with the poor.
There's a song that will linger forever in our ears, —
"Oh! hard times, come again no more."

*Chorus.* — 'Tis the song, the sigh of the weary, —
"Hard times, hard times, come again no more;
Many days you have lingered around my cabin door:
Oh! hard times, come again no more."

2.

While we seek mirth and beauty in music light and gay,
There are frail forms fainting at the door.
Though their voices are silent, their pleading looks will say,
"Oh! hard times, come again no more."

*Chorus.* — 'Tis the song, &c.

3.

'Tis a sigh that is wafted across the troubled wave;
'Tis a wail that is heard upon the shore;
'Tis a dirge that is murmured around the lowly grave, —
"Oh! hard times, come again no more."

*Chorus.* — 'Tis the song, &c.

---

## No. 6.
### Home Affections.

A COUNTRY of true homes is a country of true greatness.

A beautiful home, musical with loving voices, is the nursery of heaven.

Thou shalt rise up before the hoary-headed; thou shalt listen reverently to the wisdom of the aged; thou shalt honor thy father, and let thy words to him be full of tenderness.

Thy mother is the guardian angel of thy life: her virtues are registered indelibly upon thy heart; preserve the integrity of her good name; bless her with kindness and sympathy.

✗

Love thy brother as thou lovest thy own soul; and as often as pleasant emotions kindle to the word expressing thy relation, shalt thou feel that thou art not fighting life's battles alone and single-handed.

Thy sister is the playmate of thy youth. Let her purities be inspirations to virtue; her goodness thy emulation. If she is weak, be thou her defence; if weary, her refuge of peace.

✗

### Let us Love while we may.

*Music on page* 10.

1.

Let us love while we may: for the storms will arise,
   As we sail o'er the dim waves of time;
And the hopes of to-day may be hid from our eyes
   By the noon-clouds that darken our prime.
We may look for the lost hills of morning, and grieve;
   But the soft hush of twilight will come,
And our souls, on the rose-tinted billows of eve,
   Float calmly away to their home.

*Repeat,* — Let us love while we may, &c.

2.

Let us love while we live; and our memory will rise
   Like a halo of light from the grave,
As the day from the deep lends a glow to the eyes
   That are guarding the gloom of the wave.
There's a life in the soul that is better by far
   Than the glitter of glory or gold:
It may fade in the noon, but will shine like a star
   When the proud world is darksome and cold.

    *Repeat*, — Let us love while we may, &c.     *James G. Clark.*

---

## No. 7.

### Courage.

EVERY winter hath its spring, every ocean its glittering gems, every frost its shining crystals, every thunder-storm its compensating atmospheric purity.

Every cloud hath its silver lining, every ruin its growing vines, every wave-tossed ark its dove, every blood-stained cross its flower-wreathed crown; and for every paradise lost, there are thousands to be gained.

There is a grandeur in the soul that dares to live out all the life God lit within it.

✕
.. Bearing peace within thy soul,
   Take open ways, and brave the strife;
Dare even mockery and the scourge,
   And wear the thorny crown of life.

—

This is true courage: not the brutal force
Of vulgar heroes, but the firm resolve
Of virtue and of reason.
✕

—

Keep pushing; 'tis wiser than sitting aside,
And dreaming and sighing, and waiting the tide.
In Life's earnest battle they only prevail
Who daily march onward, and never say fail.

In life's rosy morning, in manhood's bold pride,
Let this be the motto your footsteps to guide:
" In storm and in sunshine, whatever assail,
I'll onward to conquer, and never say fail."

✗ The courage of the soldier, which makes him willing to kill or be killed, may be bought for gold; the courage which will face a wild beast in its lair is not rare: martyrs who could unflinchingly endure prison, wheel, or fagot, are not few: but that courage which denies itself for itself's own sake is rarest of all gifts, and of inestimable price. *Hudson Tuttle.*

✗ 
### The Golden Side.

*Music on page 57.*

**1.**
There is many a rest in the road of life,
If we only would stop to take it;
And many a tone from the better land,
If the querulous heart would make it.
To the sunny soul that is full of hope,
And whose beautiful trust ne'er faileth,
The grass is green and the flowers are bright,
Though the wintry storm prevaileth.

**2.**
Better hope, though the clouds o'er you hang so low;
Ever keep the sad eyes still lifted:
The sweet, sunny sky will be peeping through
When the ominous clouds are rifted.
There was ne'er a night that had not a day,
Or an evening without a morning:
The darkest hour, as the proverb goes,
Is the hour before the dawning.

**3.**
There is many a gem in the path of life,
Which we pass in our idle pleasure,
That is richer by far than the jewelled crown,
Or the miserly-hoarded treasure:
It may be the love of a little child,
Or a dear mother's prayer to heaven,
Or some lone wanderer's grateful thanks
For a cup of water given.

**4.**
Oh! 'tis better to weave in the web of life
The most beautiful golden filling,
To do all life's works with a cheerful heart,
And with hands that are swift and willing,
Than to snap the frail, tender, minute threads
Of our curious lives asunder,
And then blame Heaven for the tangled ends,
And still sit and grieve and wonder.
*Mrs. M. A. Kidder.*

---

## No. 8.

### Victory at Last.

ERROR reeleth; it staggereth like a drunken man. The windows of heaven are opened upon it, and angelic hosts assail it.
Good and evil meet and commingle upon the earth, as upon an arena for battle.

Be not affrighted; fear not.
Good shall be triumphant, and vanquish her opposing armies.
The terror of the conflict shall pass away as the cloud passeth, and sunshine and peace shall succeed it.
Quietness shall rest upon our valleys, and glory upon our mountains.

Righteousness shall flow in our streets like a river, and human hearts shall be the temples where angels dwell.
Dawn breaks through rosy billows of clouds, and glides on into a broader blaze of glory. *T. L. Harris.*

### The Old and New.

*Music on page 56.*

1.

Oh! sometimes gleams upon our sight,
Through present wrong, the eternal right;
And step by step, since time began,
We see the steady gain of man.
That all of good the past has had
Remains to make our own time glad,
Our common daily life divine,
And every land a Palestine.

2.

We lack but open eye and ear
To find the Orient's marvels here,—
The still, small voice in Autumn's hush,
Yon maple wood, the burning bush.

For still the new transcends the old,
In signs and tokens manifold:
Slaves rise up men; the olive waves
With roots deep set in battle-graves.

3.

Through the harsh notes of the day,
A low, sweet prelude finds its way;
Through clouds of doubt, and creeds of fear,
A light is breaking, calm and clear.
Henceforth my heart shall sigh no more
For olden time and holier shore:
God's love and blessing then and there
Are now, and here, and everywhere.

*J. G. Whittier.*

## No. 9.

### Scatter Roses.

IF a man say, I love God, and hateth his brother, he is a liar; for he that loveth not his brother whom he hath seen, how can he love God whom he hath not seen.

Whoever recounts to you the faults of your neighbors will doubtless expose your defects to others.

Harbor the smile of childhood in your hearts, and in old age it will halo your care-worn brow with the first glimpse of heaven.

"Give, and it shall be given unto you; good measure, pressed down, and shaken together, and running over, shall men give into your bosom."

## Let us Gather up the Sunbeams.

*Music on page 60.*

**1.**
If we knew the woe and heartache
  Waiting for us down the road,
If our lips could taste the wormwood,
  If our backs could feel the load,
Would we waste the day in wishing
  For a time that ne'er can be?
Would we wait in such impatience
  For our ships to come from sea?

**2.**
If we knew the baby-fingers
  Pressed against the window-pane
Would be cold and stiff to-morrow,
  Never trouble us again,
Would the bright eyes of our darling
  Catch the frown upon our brow?
Would the print of rosy fingers
  Vex us then as they do now?

**3.**
Ah, these little ice-cold fingers!
  How they point our memories back
To the hasty word and action,
  Strown along our backward track!
How those little hands remind us,
  As in snowy grace they lie,
Not to scatter thorns, but roses,
  For our reaping by and by!

**4.**
Let us gather up the sunbeams
  Lying all around our path;
Let us keep the wheat and roses,
  Casting out the thorns and chaff;
Let us find our sweetest comfort,
  In the blessings of to-day
With a patient hand removing
  All the briers from our way.

---

## No. 10.

### Glances Backward.

WHEN weary of looking forward into the unwrought Future, how pleasant to turn and look back into the still Past, — to the child-time of existence!

We look like fairies playing in the sunshine, in the subtile picture.

And, list! there were angels in our midst, dropping words of wisdom, teaching us lessons of integrity and bravery.

They were our fathers, our mothers, and our friends, helping us along our new way.

"The fate of the child is always the work of his mother," said the great Napoleon.

If the treachery of the world has taught us duplicity and cunning, it is well to go back and take our child-time simplicity and purity again, — our love, our faith, our expectations.

Where children are, there is the golden age.

## Childhood.

*Tune, "The Old and New."*

**1.**
Ye fairy days, when life in tune
  Played round the heart in every air,
And every note was full of love,
  And I was free from every care,

**2.**
Oft have I thought of all the joys
  Of early years so sweet and fair;
When every rose concealing thorns,
  In after-years was sere and bare;

**3.**
Whilst, in the blue of leafy June,
  As wild-birds sang their roundelay,
My senses revelled in the bloom
  That richly decked the fragrant spray.

**4.**
But now the angels from above,
  Like birds of passage, oft return;
And dewy beams of early morn
  To sunny childhood ever turn.
       *Delphia A. Carson.*

---

## No. 11.

### Liberty and Reason.

LET Truth and Falsehood grapple: who ever knew Truth put to the worst in a fair and open encounter?    *Milton.*

✗

Nature is the universal exponent of God; and reason is the eternal exponent of Nature: therefore nature and reason combined constitute the only true and reliable standard of judgment.
Obey God manifest in thyself.

✗

### Let us Live but to do what the Truth may Demand.

**1.**

*Music on page 8.*

With banners unfurled on the breezes of heaven,
  Let us press on to conquer the errors of Time;
Let us shout in the van till the welkin is riven,
  And Truth stands revealed in its beauty sublime.
Let us beard the old Error that mutters its hate,
  And curses the men who would turn to the light
The errors of churches, of parties, of state:
  Onward, push on; let us rush to the fight.

## MUSICAL READINGS.

2.

We may fall, but the banner we dauntlessly bear
  Shall fall not, but, taken by mightier hands,
Victoriously float on the dark sulphur air,
  Proclaiming the triumph of Truth's eager bands.
Let us live but to die in the struggle 'gainst wrong;
  Let us live but to do what the truth may demand:
Then Onward forever, forever! our song;
  Press on to the struggle with true heart and hand.

*Hudson Tuttle.*

---

### No. 12.

#### Childhood Morals.

NEVER kill or torture any living thing for amusement. Whoever would inflict needless suffering on the weak and helpless is a cruel tyrant and an ignominious coward. Never rob the little birds' nests of their eggs, nor mar even the wing of a butterfly. He is in ignoble business who steals from his defenceless little friends, the birds: they cannot bar their homes, nor conquer their enemies.

Be just in small things, and you will be just in great ones.

✗

Treat all playmates as equals by right. We are all brothers and sisters; and there is no high, no low, except in spiritual attainments. Be generous to make others happy, even with playthings: they are childhood's treasures.

The bud of generosity in the child will unfold into the flower of benevolence in the adult.

✗

Never throw stones at passing travellers, nor at innocent beasts or birds.
Never call any one by an unwelcome nickname.
Try, in every way you can, to make the world a good and pleasant place to yourself and others.
Laugh, frolic, dance, and be merry, but be also innocent. *J. O. Barrett.*

✗

### Be Kind to Each Other.

*From " The Psalms of Life."*

**1.**

Be kind to each other:
  The night's coming on,
When friend and when brother
  Perchance may be gone.
Then, midst our dejection,
  How sweet to have earned
The blest recollection
  Of kindness returned!

**2.**

When day hath departed,
  And memory keeps
Her watch, broken-hearted,
  Where all she loves sleeps,
Let falsehood assail not,
  Nor envy disprove;
Let trifles prevail not
  Against those you love.

**3.**

Nor change with to-morrow,
  Should fortune take wing;
But, the deeper the sorrow,
  The closer still cling.
Oh, be kind to each other!
  The night's coming on,
When friend and when brother
  Perchance may be gone.

---

## No. 13.
### I Can't and I Can.

**1.**

As on through life's journey we go day by day,
  There are two whom we meet at each turn of the way,
To help and to hinder, to bless or to ban;
And the names of these two are "*I Can't*" and "*I Can.*"

**2.**

"*I Can*" is a giant; unbending he stands:
There is strength in his arms, and skill in his hands.
He asks for no favors: he wants but a share,
Where labor is honest, and wages are fair.

**3.**

"*I Can't*" is a sluggard, too lazy to work:
From duty he shrinks; every task he will shirk.
No bread on his board, and no meal in his bag:
His house is a ruin, his coat is a rag.

**4.**

"*I Can*" is a worker: he tills the broad fields,
And digs from the earth all the wealth which it yields.
The hum of his spindles begins with the light,
And the fires of his forges are blazing all night.

##### 5.

"*I Can't*" is a coward: half fainting with fright,
At the first thought of peril he sinks out of sight;
Skulks and hides till the noise of the battle is past,
Or sells his best friends, and turns traitor at last.

##### 6.

"*I Can*" is a hero, the first in the field:
Though others may falter, he never will yield.
He makes the long marches, he deals the last blow;
His charge is the whirlwind that scatters the foe.

##### 7.

How grandly and nobly he stands to his trust!
When roused at the call of a cause that is just,
He weds his strong will to the valor of youth,
And writes on his banner the watchword of Truth.

##### 8.

Then up and be doing! the day is not long:
Throw fear to the winds; be patient and strong.
Stand fast in your place, act your part like a man,
And, when duty calls, answer promptly, "*I Can.*"

### Work is Prayer.

*From "The Psalms of Life."*

##### 1.

Brothers! be ye who ye may,
Sons of men, I bid ye pray!
Pray unceasing, pray with might,
Pray in darkness, pray in light.
Life hath yet no hours to spare:
Life is toil, and toil is prayer!

##### 2.

Life is toil; and all that lives
Sacrifice of labor gives:
Water, fire, and air and earth,
Rest not, pause not, from their birth.
Sacred toil doth nature share:
Love and labor! work is prayer.

##### 3.

Patriot! toiling for thy kind,
Thou shalt break the chains that bind;
Shape thy thought, and mould thy plan,
Toil for freedom, toil for man;
Sagely think, and boldly dare:
Labor, labor! work is prayer!

##### 4.

Brother! round thee brothers stand.
Pledge thy truth, and give thy hand;
Raise the downcast, help the weak;
Toil for good, for virtue speak.
Let thy brother be thy care:
Labor, labor! work is prayer.

*Duganne*

## No. 14.

### Peace.

WHEREFORE the wisdom of civil law, binding us to rob, maim, starve, or destroy our fellow-men? Wherefore the moral worth of a church or state that sacrifices life to preserve its authority? Wherefore the charge of guilt to him who slays only his neighbor, but the plaudits of glory to the hero who slays his thousands?

×

The life of man is sacred. There is a higher law.

×

The government is for the people, not the people for the government. Man is before and above his institutions.

×

Suffer rather than inflict suffering.
Blessed are the peacemakers; for they shall be called the children of God.

×

### Are we not Brothers?
*Music on page 53.*

1.
Hushed be the battle's fearful roar,
  The warrior's rushing call:
Why should the earth be drenched with gore?
  Are we not brothers all?

2.
Want from the starving poor, depart!
  Chains from the captive, fall!
Great God, subdue the oppressor's heart!
  Are we not brothers all?

3.
Sect, clan, and nation, oh! strike down
  Each mean partition wall;
Let love the voice of discord drown:
  Are we not brothers all?

4.
Let love and truth and peace alone
  Hold human hearts in thrall,
That Heaven its work at length may own,
  And men be brothers all.
*Mrs. Sigourney.*

---

## No. 15.

### The Hereafter.

TELL me, my soul, why art thou restless? Why dost thou look forward to the future with such strong desires?
The present is thine, and the past and the future shall be.

×

Oh, that thou didst look forward to the great hereafter with half the longing wherewith thou longest for an earthly future!
This a few days, at most, will bring thee.
Look forward to the meeting of the dead, as to the meeting of the absent.

×

Thou glorious spirit-land!
Oh that I could behold thee as thou art, — the region of life and light and love, and the dwelling-place of those whose being has flowed onward, like a silver-clear stream, into the solemn-sounding main, into the ocean of eternity! *Longfellow.*

×

Wouldst thou learn how thy spirit may enter into the delights of heaven? Learn then this lesson: —
Every noble deed of charity is heaven.
Giving water to a thirsty pilgrim is heaven.
Educating the orphan is heaven.
Watching in midnight hours with the sick, to administer the healing panacea, is heaven.
Placing a wanderer's feet in the right road is heaven.
Removing thorns and stones from a brother's or sister's pathway is heaven.
Shedding sympathy upon the unfortunate, and smiling in a brother's face, is heaven.
Lifting up the fallen, and holding them till they can stand alone, is heaven.
Leading our fellow-men into paths of virtue, and inciting them to deeds of charity, is heaven. *J. M. Peebles.*

### The Mountains of Life.

*Music on page 46.*

There's a land far away 'mid the stars, we are told,
    Where they know not the sorrows of time;
Where the pure waters wander through valleys of gold,
    And life is a treasure sublime.
'Tis the land of our God, 'tis the home of the soul,
    Where ages of splendor eternally roll,
Where the way-weary traveller reaches his goal
    On the evergreen mountains of life.

Our gaze cannot soar to that beautiful land,
    But our visions have told of its bliss;
And our souls by the gale from its gardens are fanned
    When we faint in the deserts of this.

And we sometimes have longed for its holy repose,
When our spirits were torn with temptations and woes,
And we've drank from the tide of the river that flows
  From the evergreen mountains of life.

Oh! the stars never tread the blue heavens at night,
  But we think where the ransomed have trod;
And the day never smiles from his palace of light,
  But we feel the bright smile of our God.
We are travelling homeward through changes and gloom,
To a kingdom where pleasures unceasingly bloom,
And our Guide is the glory that shines through the tomb
  From the evergreen mountains of life. *James G. Clark.*

# GOLDEN CHAIN RECITATIONS.

### No. 1.

#### Beatitudes.

*Conductor.* — Blessed are the faithful;
*Watchman.* — For they shall dwell in the confidence of men and of angels.
*Guardian of Groups.* — Blessed are the dutiful;
*Leaders.* — For they shall find the peace which cannot be bought nor sold.
*Conductor.* — Blessed are the punctual;
*Children.* — For they have learned the lesson which stars and planets teach They are students of God.
*Watchman.* — Blessed are the orderly;
*Guards.* — For theirs is the first law of progress.
*Leaders.* — Blessed are the innocent;
*Guardian of Groups.* — For they shall have peace of conscience.
*Children.* — Blessed are the pure in heart;
*Conductor.* — For they shall see God.
*Leaders.* — Blessed are the faithful, the dutiful, the punctual, the orderly, the innocent, the pure in heart;
*All.* — For theirs is the republic of heaven.

#### The World is Full of Beauty.

##### 1.

There lives a voice within me, a guest-angel of my heart;
And its sweet lispings win me till the tears a-trembling start.
Up evermore it springeth, like some magic melody,
And evermore it singeth this sweet song of songs to me:
This world is full of beauty, as other worlds above;
And, if we did our duty, it might be full of love.

**2.**

If faith and hope and kindness passed, as coin, 'twixt heart and heart,
How through the eye's tear-blindness should the sudden soul upstart!
The dreary, dim, and desolate should wear a sunny bloom,
And love should spring from buried hate like flowers from winter's tomb.
This world is full of beauty, as other worlds above;
And, if we did our duty, it might be full of love.

**3.**

With truth our uttered language, angels might talk with men,
And, God-illumined, earth should see the golden age again;
The burthened heart should soar in mirth, like morn's young prophet lark,
And misery's last tear wept on earth quench hell's last cunning spark.
The world is full of beauty, as other worlds above;
And, if we did our duty, it might be full of love.

**4.**

The leaf-tongues of the forest, and the flower-lips of the sod,
The happy birds that hymn their raptures in the ear of God,
The summer wind that bringeth music over land and sea,
Have each a voice that singeth this sweet song of songs to me:—
This world is full of beauty, as other worlds above;
And, if we did our duty, it might be full of love.

*Gerald Massey.*

## No. 2

### Invocation to the Infinite.

O INFINITE source of wisdom and love!
In the morning of my days, ere temptations have brought their sorrows, Oh teach me truth!
Give me knowledge, that I may shun the evil, and choose the good.
Let wise and loving angels guard the springs of my youth.
Let my worship be the purities of health, the strength of moral heroism, the offerings of noble thoughts, and the sacrifices of daily charities.
And may my heaven be found in the fruitions of a well-ordered life!
Hallowed be thy name!

### God Reigns in the Earth.

**1.**

Sing, sweet April blue-bird, — Oh! sing it with me, —
A pæan of joy for a land's jubilee;
And, odorous winds, on your volatile cars
Bear the freight of our rapturous song to the stars, —
 God reigns in the earth.

**2.**

Leap, stream of the woodland! charge down to the sea,
And babble the story through forest and lea;
And, gray ocean-billow, break, break, on the shore,
With a grand intonation that tells evermore,
 God reigns in the earth.

**3.**

Bend nearer, blue sky, that your clear arch may ring
And echo the jubilant anthem we sing;
Float low, angels, low, for the purified air
Of the world will not tarnish the crowns that ye wear:
 God reigns in the earth.
  *Augusta Cooper Bristol.*

---

## No. 3.

### Prayer to the Virtues.

O ANGEL of love! dwell in our bosoms as the dove of innocence.

O angel of wisdom! enlighten our understandings with the beauties thou dost unfold from spiritual affections.

O angel of justice! balance our forces of character to equalize the blessings of life.

O angel of truth! free us from false traditions and habits, and sit as a serene judge in the chambers of a clear conscience.

O angel of modesty! lead us to childhood of spirit, that we may love and cultivate the flowers of simplicity.

O angel of mercy! teach us charity and forgiveness, and breathe on us the heavenly spirit of sympathy for the suffering.

O angel of the pure in heart! hallow all our loves to holiness.

O angel of harmony! we pray for rest of soul, for thy philanthropy, for the heaven of universal peace.

O ye angels of virtue! chasten every affection of our being to love as you love the beautiful, the good, and the true.  *J. O. Barrett.*

### Better than Gold.

**1.**

Better than grandeur, better than gold,
Than rank and titles a thousand-fold,
Is a healthy body, a mind at ease,
And simple pleasures that always please;
A heart that can feel for another's woe,
And share his joys with a genial glow;
With sympathies large enough to enfold
All men as brothers, is better than gold.

**2.**

Better than gold is a conscience clear,
Though toiling for bread in an humble sphere;
Doubly blest with content and health,
Untried by the lust of cares or wealth;
Lowly living and lofty thought
Adorn and ennoble a poor man's cot.
For mind and morals, in Nature's plan,
Are the genuine test of a gentleman.

**3.**

Better than gold is the sweet repose
Of the sons of toil when their labors close;
Better than gold is the poor man's sleep,
And the balm that drops on his slumbers deep.
Bring sleeping draughts to the downy bed
Where luxury pillows his aching head :
His simple opiate labor deems
A short road to the land of dreams.

**4.**

Better than gold is a peaceful home,
Where all the fireside charities come,—
The shrine of love, the heaven of life,
Hallowed by mother or sister or wife.
However humble the home may be,
Or tried with sorrow by Heaven's decree,
The blessings that never were bought or sold
And centre there, are better than gold.

---

## No. 4.

### The Inner Judge.

| | | | |
|---|---|---|---|
| *Conductor.*— | Preserve thyself. | *Members.*— | Purify thyself. |
| " | Develop thyself. | " | Deny thyself. |
| " | Know thyself. | " | Moderate thyself. |
| " | Instruct thyself. | " | Celebrate thyself. |
| " | Affirm thyself. | " | Harmonize thyself. |

The great Judge of the world is inherent Justice.

The Supreme pierces into the recesses of the heart, as light penetrates into a dark room. We must endeavor to be in harmony with this light, like a musical instrument perfectly attuned. *Confucius.*

Behold a part of God himself within thee! Remember thine own dignity, nor dare descend to evil or meanness. *Brahimic.*

## Sun and Shadow.

**1.**

As I look from the isle, o'er its billows of green,
To the billows of foam-crested blue,
Yon bark that afar in the distance is seen,
Half dreaming, my eyes will pursue.
Now dark is the shadow, she scatters the spray,
As the chaff in the stroke of the flail;
Now white as the sea-gull, she flies on her way,
The sun gleaming bright on her sail.

**2.**

Yet her pilot is thinking of dangers to shun,
Of breakers that whiten and roar:
How little he cares, if, in shadow or sun,
They see him that gaze from the shore!

He looks to the beacon that looms from the reef,
To the rock that is under his lee,
As he drifts on the blast like a wind-wafted leaf,
O'er the gulfs of the desolate sea.

**3.**

Thus drifting afar to the dim-vaulted caves
Where life and its ventures are laid,
The dreamers who gaze while we battle the waves
May see us in sunshine or shade.
Yet true to our course, though our shadow grow dark,
We'll trim our broad sail as before,
And stand by the rudder that governs the bark,
Nor ask how we look from the shore.

*O. W. Holmes.*

---

## No. 5.

### Disappointments.

WELCOME disappointment! Thy hand is cold and hard; But it is the hand of a friend.

Thy voice is stern and harsh; but it is the voice of a friend.

Oh! there is something sublime in calm endurance.

Something sublime in the resolute fixed purpose of suffering without complaining, which makes disappointment ofttimes better than success.

Disappointments are the sunken piers upon which are rested the bridges to more rational hopes and achievements.

Then let us not drown them in thoughtless merriment.

It is a treacherous peace which is purchased by indulgence. Rather should we take them to our hearts, until we grow wiser and stronger.

Welcome, disappointment!

Thy hand is cold and hard; but it is the hand of a friend. *Longfellow.*

## Hope On, Hope Ever.

**1.**

Hope on, hope ever: though to-day be dark,
   The sweet sunburst may smile on thee to-morrow;
Though thou art lonely, there's an eye will mark
   Thy loneliness, and guerdon all thy sorrow.
Though thou must toil 'mong cold and sordid men,
   With none to echo back thy thought or love thee,
Cheer up, poor heart, thou dost not beat in vain,
   For God is over all, and heaven above thee:
      Hope on, hope ever.

**2.**

I know 'tis hard to bear the sneer and taunt,
   With the heart's honest pride at midnight wrestle,
To feel the killing canker-worm of want,
   While rich rogues in their stolen luxury nestle;
For I have felt it: yet from earth's cold real
   My soul looks out on coming things and cheerful,
The warm sunrise floods all the land ideal;
   And still it whispers to the worn and tearful,
      Hope on, hope ever.

**3.**

Hope on, hope ever: after darkest night,
   Comes, full of loving life, the laughing morning.
Hope on, hope ever: Spring-tide, flushed with light,
   Aye crowns old Winter with her rich adorning.
Hope on, hope ever; yet the time shall come
   When man to man shall be a friend and brother,
And this old world shall be a happy home,
   And all Earth's family love one another.
      Hope on, hope ever.

*Gerald Massey.*

## No. 6.
### The Religion of Health.

WHAT is our baptism?
*Frequent ablutions in pure water.*
What is our eucharist?
*Nutritious food and cold water.*
What is our inspiration?
*Plenty of sunlight and fresh air.*
What is our prayer?
*Abundant exercise.*
What is our pledge of holiness?
*Personal cleanliness.*
What is our " love-feast "?
*A clear conscience and sound sleep.*
What is our bond of fellowship?
*Sweet affections and harmonious social relations.*    **J. O. Barrett.**

### Nothing but Water to Drink.

**1.**

When the bright morning star the new daylight is bringing,
And the orchards and groves are with melody ringing,
Their way to and from them the early birds winging,
And their anthems of gladness and thanksgiving singing,
Why do they so twitter and sing, do you think?
Because they've had nothing but water to drink.

**2.**

When a shower on a hot day of summer is over,
And the fields are all smelling of white and red clover,
And the honey-bee — busy and plundering rover —
Is fumbling the blossom-leaves over and over,
Why so fresh, clean, and sweet are the fields, do you think?
Because they've had nothing but water to drink.

**3.**

Do you see that stout oak on its windy hill growing?
Do you see what great hailstones that black cloud is throwing?

Do you see that steam war-ship its ocean-way going,
Against trade-winds and head-winds, like hurricanes blowing?
Why are oaks, clouds, and war-ships so strong, do you think?
Because they've had nothing but water to drink.

### 4.

Now if WE had to work in the shop, field, or study,
And would have a strong hand, and a cheek that is ruddy,
And would NOT have a brain that is addled and muddy,
With our eyes all bunged up and our noses all bloody,
How shall WE make and keep ourselves so, do you think?
Why, WE must have nothing but water to drink. *John Pierpont.*

---

## No. 7.

### The Senses.

THY soul is the monarch of thy frame; suffer not its subjects to rebel against it.
The body is as the globe of the earth; thy bones the pillars that sustain it on its basis.

As the ocean giveth rise to springs, whose waters return again into its bosom through the rivers; so runneth thy life from the heart outwards, and so returneth it unto its place again.

Keep the currents of life pure by pure habits, and all thy being shall be healthful.

Is not thy nose the channel to perfumes? thy mouth the path to delicacies? Are not thine eyes the sentinels that watch for thee? thine ears the chambers of sound where thy soul listens enchanted?

Are not thy lungs as the winds of heaven, and thy nerves the feelers that touch the spheres of things? And all the organs of thy body and thy brain, are they not ministers of good to the inward spirit that actuates and directs all motions?

*J. O. Barrett.*

Preserve thy soul in moderation; teach thy spirit to be attentive to its good: so shall these, its ministers, be always to thee conveyances of truth.

Why, of all things living, art thou made capable of blushing? The world shall read thy shame upon thy face; therefore do nothing shameful. *Brahminic.*

## Health is Wealth.

1.

A clear bright eye
That can pierce the sky
With the strength of an eagle's vision,
And a steady brain
That can bear the strain
And shock of the world's collision;

2.

A well-knit frame,
With the ruddy flame
Aglow, and the pulses leaping
With the measured time
Of a dulcet rhyme,
Their beautiful record keeping;

3.

A rounded cheek,
Where the roses speak
Of a soil that is rich for thriving,
And a chest so grand
That the lungs expand
Exultant without the striving;

4.

A breath like morn,
When the crimson dawn
Is fresh in its dewy sweetness;
A manner bright,
And a spirit light,
With joy at its full completeness;

5.

Oh! give me these,
Nature's harmonies,
And keep all your golden treasures;
For what is wealth
To the boon of health
And its sweet attendant pleasures!

*Mrs. M. A. Kidder.*

---

## No. 8.

### Charity.

*Conductor.* — What is the bond of union?

*Leaders.* — Do unto others as ye would that others should do unto you.

*Conductor.* — What is the commandment of brotherhood?

*Officers.* — Thou shalt love thy neighbor as thyself.

*Conductor.* — What is the law of angels?

*Officers.* — All men are my brothers; all women are my sisters; all children are my children.

*Children.* — What does love require?

*Officers.* — Instruction for the ignorant, sympathy for the fallen, rest for the weary kindness to the unthankful, succor to the distressed, forgiveness to the erring.

*Guardian of Groups.* — Little children, love one another.

### Heavenly Wisdom.

Who is a wise man and endued with knowledge among you? let him show out of a good conversation his works with meekness of wisdom.

But if ye have bitter envying and strife in your hearts, glory not, and lie not against the truth.

This wisdom descendeth not from above, but is earthly, sensual, devilish.

For where envying and strife is, there is confusion and every evil work.

But the wisdom that is from above is first pure, then peaceable, gentle, and easy to be entreated, full of mercy and good fruits, without partiality, and without hypocrisy.

And the fruit of righteousness is sown in peace of them that make peace.

---

## No. 9.

### The Unity and Eternity of Labor.

WHAT a glorious thing is human life!
How glorious man's destiny!
We behold all round about us, one vast union.
No man can labor for himself,
Without laboring at the same time for all others.
This truth becomes an inward benediction, lifting the soul mightily upward.
The feeling of our dignity and power grows strong when we say:
Being is not objectless and vain; we all are necessary links in the great chain which reaches forward into eternity.

All the great and wise and good whose names we read in the world's history have labored for us.
We have entered into their harvest.
We tread in their footsteps from which blessings grow.
We can undertake the sublime task which they once undertook.
We can try to make our common brotherhood wiser and happier.
We can build forward where they were forced to leave off,
And bring nearer to perfection the great edifice which they left uncompleted.
And at length we, too, must leave it and go hence.

Oh! this is the sublimest thought of all.
We can never finish the noble task of life.

We can never cease to work, we can never cease to be.
What men call death cannot break off this task, which is never-ending.
No period is set to our being: we are eternal.
We lift our heads boldly to the threatening mountain-peaks, and to the roaring cataract, and to the storm-clouds swimming in the fire-sea overhead, and say,
    We are eternal, and defy your power. Break, break over us!
And thou Earth, and thou Heaven,
Mingle in the wild tumult!
And ye Elements, foam and rage and destroy these atoms of dust,—
These bodies we call ours!
Spirit, with its fixed purpose, shall hover brave and triumphant over the ruins of the universe.
For it is eternal.     *Longfellow.*

## The Web of Life.

**1.**

I thought to call thee Heaviness, O Life! whose name is Lightness.
  I said, "Thy pulse is bitterness," O Heart of honey sweet!
When a sphere revolves in darkness, doth it know its central brightness?
  When the ages seem abortive, can the moments be complete?

**2.**

I was weary, more than weary, on a sultry summer morning,
  As I filled Life's busy shuttle with Duty's iron thread:
"Though the sum of my achievement all the world should hold in scorning,
  If the Over-Soul approveth, I am content," I said.

**3.**

"If the Over and the Under and the Inner Soul approveth,
  The great encircling Unity, the central All in All,
I will sing despite my faintness, for the sake of Him who loveth,
  The frail things and the tender, the weak things and the small."

**4.**

The golden thread of human love, full well had it been proven;
  I never have forgotten quite the rainbows that it made;
But alas for all the failure of the web when it was woven!
  The shame of noting, day by day, the glowing colors fade.

#### 5.

How my spirit flamed within me, in a grand and frantic fashion !
    I tore the mesh, and trampled on the falsely shining thread,
Till I rose serene and patient from the ashes of my passion,
    And flung the busy shuttle of Reality instead.

#### 6.

I gave no ear to Fancy, and I dallied not for Beauty,
    And faint as whispering echoes the voice of Pleasure rang;
For me, I only cared to hear the clarion of Duty,
    And work my rhythmic treadles to the trumpet-song she sang.

#### 7.

On that sultry summer morning, something held me in its keeping,
    For a stupor came upon me, and I fancy that I slept;
But the web of Life went onward, through the dreaming and the sleeping,
    And my weak hands at the shuttle their rhythmic movement kept.

#### 8.

And I thought celestial voices murmured down the ether spaces,
    And angel wings came noiselessly and stirred the summer air;
And behind a cloud of glory were the loving spirit faces,
    And their talk with one another was a music sweet and rare.

#### 9.

" She endureth and is faithful; " (low and tenderly they spake it;)
    " She endureth and is patient, and she maketh no complaint;
She knoweth not the tapestry she weaveth; let us take it,
    And reveal it to her vision, for her spirit groweth faint.

#### 10.

" She prayeth not for pity, yet her heart delighteth ever
    In the kindly deed of mercy and the loving sacrifice;
Then let us gather up the sombre web of her endeavor,
    And in the true celestial light unfold it to her eyes."

#### 11.

Then soft they floated downward, and they spread before my vision
    The web that I had woven, yet never turned to see;
Oh! the harpers and the seraphim that walk the field elysian,
    That moment must have shouted a song of praise for me.

### 12.

A universe alone could voice my triumph and my gladness;
  For lo, the work my hand had wrought, through weariness and cold,
Was not a sombre tracery upon a ground of sadness,
  But beds of sweetest bloom embossed upon a field of gold.

### 13.

And there were living roses, for their golden censers swinging
  Were filled with honey-wine, embalming all the summer air;
And birds with burnished plumage were 'mong the blossoms singing,
  And butterflies on wings of golden flame were rocking there.

### 14.

Then suddenly I wakened with the rapture and the wonder,
  And life was glory. I had read the riddle of its task:
For the gold of Love Eternal is around, above, and under;
  And who or what is Duty, but Love's angel in a mask?

*Augusta Cooper Bristol.*

---

## No. 10.

### True Womanhood.

LO! yonder standeth the house of joy. Within, an angel walketh in maiden sweetness, with innocence in her mind, and modesty on her cheek.

On her tongue dwelleth music; the sweetness of honey floweth from her lips.

Her eye speaketh softness and love, and discretion with a sceptre sitteth on her brow. The tongue of the licentious is dumb in her presence; the awe of her virtue keepeth him silent.

When scandal is busy, the finger of silence resteth on her lip.

Her breast is the mansion of purity and goodness;

Therefore she suspecteth no evil in others.

Happy is the man that shall make her his wife.

Happy is the son that shall call her mother. *Brahminic.*

## When this old Earth is Righted.

### 1.

I searched the volume of my heart,
I spread its purple lids apart,
Its leaves with inspiration's art,
   And prophecy indited.
Entranced with trope and mystic rhyme,
I caught the symphony sublime,
The prelude of the coming time:
   I saw the old Earth righted.

### 2.

Thou shalt lay cross and burden down,
Humanity, and take thy crown,
The bride of Heaven in lily gown,
   With every wrong requited;
Enthroned for thy achievement vast,
With each ideal of the past
One grand reality at last,
   When this old Earth is righted.

### 3.

And nations shall not then, as now,
The cause of righteousness avow,
With "ego" written on the brow;
   But each to each united
Shall wear the badge of sacrifice,
And drop the hypocrite's disguise,
And face high Heaven with honest eyes,
   When this old Earth is righted.

### 4.

No more before Redemption's gate,
Stumbling at prejudice and hate,
Humanity shall hesitate,
   To Liberty half plighted;
For truths that loosely lie apart
Shall be inwrought into the heart
By Reason's skill and Wisdom's art,
   When this old Earth is righted.

### 5.

And Freedom's march no more shall pause
At God Almighty's broken laws.
The full requirements of her cause
   Shall nevermore be slighted:
Nor civic strategy elude
Equality and brotherhood;
And Justice shall pronounce it good
   When this old Earth is righted.

### 6.

And woman's life no more shall be
The playground of hypocrisy,
But earnest, natural, and free:
   And Love shall stay unfrighted,
And reign in sacred, sweet content,
And offer service reverent;
For marriage shall be sacrament
   When this old Earth is righted.

### 7.

Then urge thy tardy courser, Time!
We watch to hail the blessed prime,
We listen for the morning chime
   That heralds the long-plighted:
Humanity and the Divine
Shall wed at Nature's sacred shrine,
Completing Infinite design,
   When this old Earth is righted.

              *Augusta Cooper Bristol.*

---

## No. 11.

### A Ladder of Light.

WHAT is the first step towards progress?
   *A desire to know and follow truth.*
What is the second step?
*A willingness to receive it, without dictating how it shall come.*

What is the third step?
*Courage to cherish and defend it, making it a part of our lives.*
What law of progress ought we always to remember?
*Fraternal love. We should do as we would be done by.*
What is the first lesson in fraternal love?
*Faith in our fellow-beings; faith that there is in every human soul a desire to be good.*
What does this faith teach us?
*Charity, which covereth a multitude of sins; that sins flow from weakness and imperfection, and we pity where we cannot blame.*
Does charity necessitate toleration?
*"The greatest good of the greatest number," should be the motto of nations and individuals.*
What is the grand ultimate of truth?
*The truth shall make you free.*

Emma Tuttle.

## Voices.

Heir of an infinite privilege, with earnest zeal I wrought,
And gathered the true and the beautiful to the glowing forge of thought.

And there in the vital furnace heat, full patiently and long,
I changed my wealth, in a human way, to deed and simple song.

And there came a voice from the world without,—oh! very sweet with praise,
And the waft that bore it seemed the breath of freshly-woven bays.

And my soul was glad for a moment, in that little breeze of fame,
Though a shadow darkened the purity of the living central flame;

But the Heavens, that loved my loyalty, encompassed me around,
Till my spirit ear was opened, and I heard the wondrous sound

Of far majestic voices behind the sunset bars,
And sweet and mighty utterances between the solemn stars;

Till, awed to a nobler faithfulness, and humbled very low,
I wrought again at the forge of thought, since God would have it so.

Yet howe'er weak or imperfect the deed and the rhythmic song,
I crowned for aye the eternal Right, and branded the ancient Wrong.

And lo, a voice from the world again! and oh! it was dread with blame:
The waft that bore it like a breath from poisonous ivy came.

And my soul sank down a moment, bewildered with a doubt,
And the phantom of Misgiving was brooding round about.

But the Heavens, that loved my loyalty, unsealed my ear again;
And I heard the sound of voices, soft and low as summer rain.

A voice through all the emerald spires where meadow-grasses grow,
A colloquy between the leaves where summer roses blow.

A voice from the fairy chamber, behind the sea-shell's lip,
And a whisper among the mosses where woodland rivulets slip.

A voice from the swaying lilies among the river reeds,
An oracle faintly sighing up from the root to the golden seeds.

A voice that the swinging butterfly folds under its downy wings,
And a low, miraculous murmur from the soul of creeping things.

And the prophecy of the joint refrain, the theme of the tiny whole,
Was a hint of the infinite value of the earnest human soul.

Then, saved by the mystic murmurings from over-pride or shame,
I wrought again, in my simple way, secure from praise or blame.

And between the voices far and high, and whisperings near and low,
I live for the true and the beautiful, for God would have it so.

*Augusta Cooper Bristol.*

## No. 12.
### Esteem Thyself.

WHAT should be the first ambition of every one?
    *To command his own esteem. One cannot retain the esteem of others who is not worthy of his own.*
Is self-esteem vanity?
    *No. It is the consciousness of having lived righteously.*
Can we esteem ourselves when we cheat and deceive our fellow-beings?
    *No. We feel that we do not deserve trust. We grow weak, faltering, and unsafe.*
How can we best gain our own esteem?
    *By being honest in our dealings, truthful in the utterance of our opinions, brave in vindicating them when assailed, and courageous in living them, always testing their merits by their results.*
    *Emma Tuttle.*

### Live Righteously.

" So live, that when thy summons comes to join
The innumerable caravan that moves
To that mysterious realm where each shall take
His chamber in the silent halls of death,
Thou go not, like the quarry-slave at night,
Scourged to his dungeon; but sustained and soothed
By an unfaltering trust, approach thy grave,
Like one who wraps the drapery of his couch
About him, and lies down to pleasant dreams."
William C. Bryant.

### The Strength of the Faithful.

Let Fate or Insufficiency provide
Mean ends for men who what they are would be:
Penned in their narrow day, no change they see
Save death, which strikes the blow to brutes and pride.
Our faith is ours, and comes not on a tide;
And whether earth's great offspring, by decree,
Must rot if they abjure rapacity,
Not argument but effort shall decide.
They number many heads in that hard flock;
Trim swordsmen they push forth; yet try thy steel!
Thou, fighting for poor human-kind, wilt feel
The strength of Roland in thy wrist to hew
A chasm sheer into the barrier rock,
And bring the army of the faithful through.

---

## No. 13.

### The Kingdoms of Nature.

WHAT is the lowest kingdom in nature?
*The mineral.*
What is the name of that kingdom immediately above the mineral?
*The vegetable.*
What is next above the vegetable?
*The animal.*

What above the animal?
*The human.*
What rises above the human, the highest and most glorious of all?
*The spiritual.*
What do you mean by the mineral kingdom?
*The base of the grand pyramid of existence.*
What do you mean by the vegetable kingdom?
*The first step of this pyramid, wrought by the action of living forces.*
What do you mean by the animal kingdom?
*The second step, including the vast domain from the beginning of sentient life to the bounds of the human.*
What do you mean by the human kingdom?
*The third step, on which man stands alone, as the representative of developed reason and intellect, and prophecy of immortality.*
What do you mean by the spiritual kingdom?
*The infinite apex, the crowning glory of Life's grand pyramid; the region of infinite force, and the destination of all progress.* Hudson Tuttle.

---

## No. 14.

### Matter and Spirit.

WHAT are the two great divisions of nature?
*Matter and spirit.*
What is matter?
*The material of which every thing is made.*
What is spirit?
*It is a pure and eternal force.*
Of what is matter composed?
*Atoms.*
What is an atom?
*It is the indivisible centre from which force emanates.*
What are the three states of matter?
*Solid, liquid, and gaseous.*
How do we learn the qualities of matter?
*By means of its emanating force or spirit.*
Do we know any thing of matter except by means of its forces?
*It is unseen, unfelt, and unknown.*
Will you illustrate this grand truth?
*As we learn of the sun by means of its light, heat, and gravitation, so do we learn of the atom by its attraction, methods of combination and other qualities. When we come in*

*contact with a solid, it is not the atom we touch, we only touch the sphere of its emanating force.*
What is the relation between matter and force?
*They are inseparable, co-existent, and co-eternal.*           Hudson Tuttle.

## No. 15.

### The Three Rules.

WHAT is the lowest rule of human conduct?
*The Iron Rule.*
What is the next higher rule?
*The Silver Rule.*
What is the highest rule of human conduct?
*The Golden Rule.*
What is the Iron Rule?
*Evil for evil.*
What is the Silver Rule?
*Good for good.*
What is the Golden Rule?
*Good for evil.*
Why do you consider the Iron Rule the lowest?
*Because it is the expression of the animal faculties of the mind, and the law of brutes and savages.*
Why is the Silver Rule better?
*Because it is the Golden Rule half expressed.*
Why is the Golden Rule the highest and the best?
*Because it is the essence of our spiritual perception of right; and, flowing from the highest faculties of our nature, must be the best guide in the conduct of life.*

## No. 16.

### The True and the False.

ANSWER, O soul! What is the sweetest and best of all things?
*Love.*
What is the worst?
*Cruelty.*

Answer, O soul! what is the noblest of all things?
*To do our duty.*
What is the basest?
*To be treacherous towards others.*
Answer, O soul! What is the grandest of all things?
*The divine mind.*
What is the meanest?
*An envious disposition.*
Answer, O soul! What is the purest of all things?
*Charity.*
What is the foulest?
*A slanderous tongue.*
Answer, O soul! what is the most beautiful of all things?
*A good life.*
What is the ugliest?
*A deformed spirit.*
Answer, O soul! what is the wisest of all things?
*Adherence to truth.*
What is the most foolish?
*Vanity.*
Answer, O soul! what is the rarest of all things?
*A mind which is purely self-sustaining.*
What is the most pleasing of all things?
*A contemplation of all God's excellencies.*
What is the most distressing?
*The contemplation of Vice and her attendant evils.*

Mrs. E. S. Ledsham.

## Invocation to our Divinities.

### 1.

O Spirit of Light! may the time hasten on,
When wronging and crime from our midst shall have gone,
And the gospel of angels, throughout the broad land,
Like a beautiful bride at our home-altars stand!

### 2.

O Spirit of Peace! may the dark waves subside
That dash us about on contention's fierce tide,
And warring winds hush at the fiat of will,
That speaks to the soul of the rocker, "Be still!"

#### 3.

O Spirit of Love! with thy magical wand
Touch sweetly each heart in our sin-shrouded land,
And make, with thy roseate tintings of light,
The sable-hued garments of mortals more bright.

#### 4.

O Spirit of Truth! may the sound of thy feet,
Like the firm tread of armies that know not defeat,
Be heard in our land; and thy strong arm of might
Be lifted to aid those who stand for the right.

#### 5.

O Spirit of Man! bound in fetters of clay,
While swiftly the moments of time flee away.
Work hard for all truth while those brief moments last,
That thy life may be sweet when the earth-shores are past.

*Mrs. M. J. Kutz*

---

## No. 17.
### Life Builders.

#### 1.

HOW the busy builders throng!
Ever coming, ever going,
Day by day their great walls growing,
To the hammer's ringing song.
Whether reared on Fashion's highway,
Or on close and crowded by-way,
Still are homes for men upspringing,
Still is Labor's anthem ringing,
Where the workman plays his part,
Stout of hand and true of heart.

#### 2.

Thus, with deeper meaning fraught,
Viewless mansions all are rearing,
On their shadowy walls appearing
All the work our hands have wrought.
Though we build for song or story,
Carve out cross or crown of glory,
Silently and very slowly
Build we on foundations lowly
Laid with word, or deed, or pen,
Hidden in the hearts of men.

#### 3.

Therefore should you build, my friend,
Nobly, with high scorn refusing
Low aims offered for the using,
Doubtful ways to some good end.
Write above life's archway golden,
These strong words of knighthood olden,
*"Better stony truths unfearing*
*Than a lie with smooth veneering;*
*Richer Honor's empty purse*
*Than a pilfered universe."*

#### 4.

Lay foundations deep and wide,
Not on white sands idly drifting,
But upon the rocks, uplifting
All their grandeur o'er the tide;
Build so wide that every other
Struggling soul shall be your brother.
Light a beacon for the weary,
Toiling long through darkness dreary,
That your towers may stand complete,
Crowned with benedictions sweet.

#### 5.

Let your works be fair to see, —
Trace the lines of grace and beauty
Round the rugged front of duty;
And, where'er your lot may be, —
Wayside tent, or marble palace,
Cottage girt about with lilies, —
Make life something worth the living,
Use God's gifts, whate'er the giving;
And his record pure shall tell
You have builded true and well.

#### 6.

Build your mansion sure, my friend, —
From foundation-stone to rafter
Build it for the vast hereafter,
Making strength and beauty blend
Like a hint of grace supernal,
Like a dream of domes eternal,
Where the shafts of sunrise quiver
O'er the homes beyond the river,
On the streets by angels trod,
In the city of our God.

*Annie Herbert.*

## No. 18.

### The Dawn of Redemption.

#### 1.

SEE them go forth like the floods to the ocean,
   Gathering might from each mountain and glen,
Wider and deeper the tide of devotion
   Rolls up to God from the bosoms of men.
Hear the great multitude, mingling in chorus,
   Groan as they gaze from their crimes to the sky, —
"Father, the midnight of death gathers o'er us;
   When will the dawn of redemption draw nigh?"

#### 2.

Look on us, wanderers, sinful and lowly,
   Struggling with grief and temptation below;
Thine is the goodness o'er every thing holy,
   Thine is the mercy to pity our woe;
Thine is the power to cleanse and restore us,
   Spotless and pure as the angels on high, —
"Father, the midnight of death gathers o'er us;
   When will the dawn of redemption draw nigh?"

#### 3.

Gray hair and golden youth, matron and maiden,
   Lovers of mammon and followers of fame,
All with the same solemn burden are laden,
   Lifting their souls to that one mighty name.

Wild is the pathway that surges before us;
  On the broad waters the black shadows lie.
"Father, the midnight of death gathers o'er us·
  When will the dawn of redemption draw nigh?"

### 4.

Lo! the vast depths of futurity's ocean
  Heave with the pulse of the Infinite breath:
Why should we shrink at the billow's commotion?
  Angels are walking the waters of death;
Angels are mingling with men in the chorus
  Rising like incense from earth to the sky, —
"Father, the billows grow brighter before us:
  Heaven, with its mansions eternal, draws nigh."

J. G. Clark.

## No. 19

### Drop Charity's Curtain.

#### 1.

DROP the white curtain.
  O friends! be certain
Never was hurt in
  Forgiveness and love.
Throw down your lances,
Soften your glances,
Reason advances
  With words from above.
When Sin pauses, weeping,
In humbleness creeping
To Charity's keeping,
  What action is best?
Curses to fling to her?
Censures to bring to her?
  Or pity and rest?

#### 2.

Weak heart and strong heart,
Good heart and wrong heart,
Have felt the long smart
  Which wrong-doing brings.
All mortals cover
Some blemish over,
Though you discover
  No pain-throbbing stings.

We are all brothers,
Clay-formed our mothers,
Each, like all others,
  Too much to forget.
We must have our time,
Facing the shower-time,
  Cold, pleading, and wet.

#### 3.

Men may cry, "Stranger!
Whence came you, ranger?
Through what grim danger
  That made you so black?"
But they know well enough
Where lie the passes rough:
They blacked a glove and cuff
  Who passed the same track.
Pharisee! blame him!
Point at him! shame him!
Shun and disclaim him,
  Through nights and through days.
God knoweth both of you:
Clear as a globe of dew
  He sees all your ways.

4.

Envy! Peace-scarer!
Black thunder-bearer!
Would you were rarer
    Than white angels be!
When will Time's surges
Bury your scourges
Too deep for dirges
    To sound down the sea?
When on man's growing
Love's breath is blowing,
And life is flowing
    In sight of its God,
Feet treading under
Tempest and thunder,
    Pass under the rod.

5.

Drop the white curtain.
O friends! be certain
Never was hurt in
    Forgiveness and love.
Broken hearts bleed for it,
Ashen lips plead for it,
We all have need for it,
    Vulture and dove.
Oh! when wild demons cry,
Till all our angels fly,
Leaving us hell to eye,
    Pallid with fear,—
Drop the white curtain:
Never was hurt in
    A pitying tear.
        *Emma Tuttle.*

## No. 20.

### The Beautiful Land.

1.

THERE'S a beautiful land by the spoiler untrod,
    Unpolluted by sorrow or care.
It is lighted alone by the presence of God,
    Whose throne and whose temple are there;
Its crystalline streams, with a murmurous flow,
    Meander through valleys of green;
And its mountains of jasper are bright in the glow
    Of a splendor no mortal hath seen.

2.

And throngs of glad singers, with jubilant breath,
    Make the air with their melodies rife;
And one known on earth as the angel of death
    Shines here as the angel of life.
And infinite tenderness beams from his eyes;
    On his brow is an infinite calm;
And his voice, as it thrills through the depth of the skies,
    Is as sweet as the seraphim's psalm.

### 3.

Through the amaranth groves of a beautiful land
  Walk the souls who were faithful in this;
And their foreheads, star-crowned, by the zephyrs are fanned,
  That evermore murmur of bliss.
They taste the rich fruitage that hangs from the trees,
  And breathe the sweet odor of flowers,
More fragrant than ever were kissed by the breeze
  In Araby's loveliest bowers.

### 4.

Old prophets, whose words were a spirit of flame,
  Blazing out o'er the darkness of time;
And martyrs, whose courage no torture could tame,
  Nor turn from their purpose sublime;
And saints and confessors, a numberless throng,
  Who were loyal to truth and to right,
And left, as they walked through the darkness of wrong,
  Their footprints encircled with light.

### 5.

And the dear little children who went to their rest
  Ere their lives had been sullied by sin,
While the angel of morning still tarried a guest,
  Their spirits' pure temple within.
All are there, all are there, in the beautiful land,
  The land by the spoiler untrod;
And their foreheads, star-crowned, by the breezes are fanned,
  That blow from the gardens of God.

### 6.

My soul hath looked in through the gateway of dreams,
  On the city all paved with gold,
And heard the sweet flow of its murmurous streams,
  As through the green valleys they rolled;
And though it still waits on this desolate strand,
  A pilgrim and stranger on earth,
Yet it knew, in that glimpse of the beautiful land,
  That it gazed on the home of its birth.

## No. 21.

### Life's Roses.

**1.**

WHEN the morning first uncloses,
   And before the mists are gone,
All the hills seem bright with roses,
   Just a little farther on, —
Roses red as wings of starlings,
   And with diamond dew-drops wet.
"Wait," says Patience, "wait, my darlings,
   Wait a little longer yet!"
So, with eager, upturned faces,
   Wait the children for the hours
That shall bring them to the places
   Of the tantalizing flowers.

**2.**

Wild with wonder, sweet with guesses,
   Vexed with only fleeting fears,
So the broader day advances,
   And the twilight disappears.
Hands begin to clutch at posies,
   Eyes to flash with new delight;
And the roses, — oh! the roses,
   Burning, blushing, full in sight.

**3.**

Now with bosoms softly beating,
   Heart in heart, and hand in hand,
Youths and maids, together meeting,
   Crowd the flowery harvest-land.
Nor a thought of rainy weather,
   Nor of thorns to sting and grieve:
Gather, gather, gather, gather;
   All the care is what to leave.

**4.**

Noon to afternoon advances;
   Rosy red grows russet brown;
Sad eyes turn to backward glances,
   So the sun of youth goes down.
And, as rose by rose is withered,
   Sober sight begins to find
Many a false heart has been gathered,
   Many a true one left behind.
Hands are clasped with fainter holding,
   Unfilled souls begin to sigh
For the golden, glad unfolding
   Of the morn beyond the sky.
               *Alice Cary.*

---

## No. 22.

### Trust to the Future.

**1.**

TRUST to the future. Though, gloomy and cheerless,
   Prowls the dark past like a shade at thy back,
Look not behind thee; be hopeful and fearless;
   Steer for the right way, and keep to the track.
Fling off despair, it hath strength like a giant;
   Shoulder thy purpose, and, boldly defiant,
Save to the right, stand unmoved and unpliant:
   Faith and God's promise the brave never lack.

### 2.

Trust to the future. The present may fright thee,
  Scowling so fearfully close at thy side :
Face it unmoved, and no present can blight thee;
  He who stands boldly each blast shall abide.
Never a storm but the tainted air needs it;
Never a storm but the sunshine succeeds it :
Each has a lesson ; and he alone reads it
  Rightly, who takes it, and makes it his guide.

### 3.

Trust to the future : it stands like an angel,
  Waiting to lead thee, to bless, and to cheer ;
Singing of hope like some blessed evangel,
  Luring thee on to a brighter career.
Why should the past or the present oppress thee ?
Stamp on their coils ; for, with arms to caress thee,
See, the great future stands yearning to bless thee :
  Press boldly forward, nor yield to a fear.

### 4.

Trust to the future : it will not deceive thee,
  So thou but meet it with brave heart and strong.
Now begin living anew, and, believe me,
  Gladness and triumph will follow ere long.
Never a night but there cometh a morrow ;
Never a grief but the hopeful will borrow
Something of gladness to lighten the sorrow :
  Life unto such is a conqueror's song.

## No. 23.

### The Spirit World.

### 1.

THE spirit-world around this world of sense
  Floats like an atmosphere, and everywhere
Wafts through these earthly mists and vapors dense
  A vital breath of more ethereal air.

### 2.

Our little lives are kept in equipoise
  By opposite attractions and desires:
The struggle of the instinct that enjoys,
  And the more noble instinct that aspires.

### 3.

These perturbations, this perpetual jar
  Of earthly wants, and aspirations high,
Come from the influence of an unseen star,
  An undiscovered planet in our sky.

### 4.

And as the moon from some dark gate of cloud
  Throws o'er the sea a floating bridge of light,
Across whose trembling planks our fancies crowd
  Into the realms of mystery and night;

### 5.

So, from the world of spirits there descends
  A bridge of light connecting it with this,
O'er whose unsteady floor, that sways and bends,
  Wander our thoughts above the dark abyss.  *Longfellow.*

---

## No. 24.

### "Peace, Perfect Peace."

#### 1.

WHERE may perfect peace be found?
  Can we find it in the grave?
No: the green embroidered mound
  Where the lowly grasses wave
Doth not rest the weary soul
  In its silence dark and deep;
For Death's melancholy toll
  Only lays the form to sleep.

#### 2.

Where may perfect peace be found?
  For the spirit cannot die,
Nor lie dreamless in the ground
  As the last year's roses lie.

In the clustered gems of earth,—
  Diamonds, garnets, opals, pearls?
Brilliants are of little worth,
  Save to signal kings and earls.

#### 3.

Where may perfect peace be found?
  In the dower which beauty gives?
No: the head with graces crowned
  Bows and fades and vanishes;
Bears its griefs and braves its pains,
  Dreaming of a perfect rest;
Mourns its losses, counts its gains,
  Rosaries upon the breast.

#### 4.

Where may perfect peace be found?
 In the laurel-leaves of fame,
Wherewith mighty men are crowned
 When the peoples shout a name?
No, not there: for crowning leaves
 Soon grow faded, crisp, and brown;
And thought's roaring ocean heaves
 New names up and beats old down.

#### 5.

Where may perfect peace be found?
 Tell us, O ye guides above!
"Perfect peace?' she sitteth crowned
 In the soul replete with love."
There, serene 'mid clash and jars
 Dwelling in earth's twilight even,
She can pass the tomb's dark bars,
 And live on for aye in heaven.

*Emma Tuttle.*

## No. 25.

### The Voice of Progress.

#### 1.

CAN ye lengthen the hours of the dying night,
 Or chain the wings of the morning light?
Can ye seal the springs of the ocean deep,
Or bind the thunders in silent sleep?
 The sun that rises, the seas that flow,
 The thunders of heaven, all answer, No!

#### 2.

Can ye drive young Spring from the blossomed earth,
The earthquake still in its awful birth?
Will the hand on Time's dial backward flee,
Or the pulse of the universe pause for thee?
 The shaken mountains, the flowers that blow,
 The pulse of the Universe, answer, No!

#### 3.

Can ye burn a truth in the martyr's fire,
Or chain a thought in the dungeon dire?
Or stay the soul when it soars away,
In glorious life from the mouldering clay?
 The truth that liveth, the thoughts that grow,
 The spirit ascending, all answer, No!

4.

O priest! O despot! *your doom* they speak;
For God is mighty, as ye are weak.
Your night and your winter from earth must roll,
Your chains must melt from the limb and soul.
    Ye have wrought us wrong, ye have brought us woe:
    Shall ye triumph much longer? we answer, No!

5.

Ye have builded your temples with gems impearled;
On the broken heart of a famished world.
Ye have crushed its heroes in desert graves,
Ye have made its children a race of slaves.
    O'er the future age shall the ruin go?
    We gather against ye, and answer, No!

6.

Ye laugh in scorn from your shrines and towers;
But weak are ye, for the *truth* is ours.
In arms, in gold, and in pride ye move;
But we are stronger, *our strength is love.*
    Can truth be slain with a curse or blow?
    The beautiful heavens, they answer, No!

7.

The wintry night of the world is past,
The day of humanity dawns at last;
The veil is rent from the soul's calm eyes,
And prophets and heroes and seers arise.
    Their words and deeds like the thunder go:
    Can ye stifle their voices? they answer, No.

8.

It is God who speaks in their words of might;
It is God who acts in their deeds of right.
Lo! Eden waits, like a radiant bride:
Humanity springeth close to her side.
    Can ye sever the twain who to oneness flow?
    The voice of Divinity answers, No.

## No. 26.

### A Moral Code.

MEN are made for each other; even the inferior for the sake of the superior, and these for the sake of one another.
Invincible influences are exerted on men, and mould their opinions and acts.
Sin is error and ignorance, — an involuntary slavery.
We are ourselves feeble, and by no means immaculate; and often our very abstinence from faults is due more from cowardice, and care of our reputation, than to any freedom from the disposition to commit them.
Our judgments are very rash, and apt to be premature. "And, in short, a man must learn a great deal to enable him to pass a correct judgment on another man's acts."
When much vexed or grieved, consider that a man's life is only a moment, and after a short time we are all dead.
No wrongful act of another can bring shame on us; and it is not men's acts which disturb us, but our own opinion of them.
Our own anger hurts us more than the acts of themselves.
Benevolence is invincible, if it be not an affected smile, nor acting a part. For what will the most violent man do if you continue benevolent to him, gently and calmly correcting him, admonishing him when he is trying to do you harm, saying, "Not so, child: we are constituted by nature for something else. I shall certainly not be injured; but thou art injuring thyself, my child." *Marcus Aurelius.*

Ever hold in remembrance this talismanic sentiment, making it a part of your being: My country is the universe; my home is the world; my religion to do good; my heaven wherever a human heart beats in harmony with mine.
*J. M. Peebles.*

---

## No. 27.

### Spirit Hunger.

**1.**

COME to me, angels! the room of my spirit
    Is garnished and swept for a season by prayer:
I have cast out, just to win you anear it,
    All the earth-vanities brooding in there.
        Come to me, angels!
    Lift for a moment my curtain of care.

2.

I am so weary of earthly supineness, —
   Life that is levelled to labor and pay;
I am so hungry for Nature's divineness,
   Hungry to talk with her just for a day.
      Come to me, angels!
Write in my heart the sweet words she would say.

3.

Bear on your wings, in your coming and going,
   Wafts of her breathings o'er prairie and lea;
Bring me sweet hints, from the May roses blowing,
   Of Deity's thoughts sprung to bloom on a tree.
      Come to me, angels!
Tell what the roses are keeping for me.

4.

Open to me, by a sacred impressment,
   Mysteries hid in a gurgle of song,
Secrets enfolded in purple caressment
   Close in the tubes where the honey-bees throng.
      Come to me, angels!
Bearing the bird and bee message along.

*Augusta Cooper Bristol.*

## No. 28.

### Voices of the Past and Future.

1.

A WAILING voice came up a desolate road,
   Drearily, drearily, drearily!
Where mankind have trodden the by-way of blood,
   Wearily, wearily, wearily!
Like a sound of the Dead Sea, all shrouded in glooms;
   With breaking of hearts, fetters clanking, men groaning,
Or chorus of ravens, that croak among tombs,
   It comes with the mournfullest moaning:
      "Weep, weep, weep!"

Yoke-fellows, listen
Till tearful eyes glisten :
'Tis the voice of the Past, — the dark, grim-featured Past,
All sad as the shriek of the midnight blast.
Weep, weep, weep !
Tears to wash out the red, red stain,
Where life ran a deluge of hot, bloody rain,
Weep, weep, weep !

2.

There cometh another voice sweetest of all,
Cheerily, cheerily, cheerily !
And my heart leapeth up at its glorious call,
Merrily, merrily, merrily !
It comes like the soft touch of spring-tide, unwrapping
The thrall of oppression that bound us ;
It comes like a choir of the seraphim, harping
Their gladsomest music around us, —
" Hope, hope, hope ! "
Yoke-fellows, listen
Till tearful eyes glisten :
'Tis the voice of the Future, the sweetest of all,
That makes the heart leap to its glorious call.
Hope, hope, hope !
Brothers, step forth in the Future's van,
For the worst is past :
Right conquers at last,
And the better day dawns upon suffering man.
Hope, hope, hope !  *Gerald Massey.*

## No. 29.

### Flowers.

1.

SPAKE full well, in language quaint and olden,
One who dwelleth by the castled Rhine,
When he called the flowers, so blue and golden,
Stars that in earth's firmament do shine.

2.

Stars they are wherein we read our history,
    As astrologers and seers of old;
Yet not wrapped about with awful mystery,
    Like the burning stars which they behold.

3.

Wondrous truths, and manifold as wondrous,
    God hath written in those stars above;
But not less in the bright flow'rets under us
    Stands the revelation of his love.

4.

Bright and glorious is that revelation,
    Written all over this great world of ours;
Making evident our own creation
    In these stars of earth, — these golden flowers.

5.

And the poet, faithful and far-seeing,
    Sees, alike in stars and flowers, a part
Of the self-same universal being
    Which is throbbing in his brain and heart.

6.

Gorgeous flow'rets in the sunlight shining,
    Blossoms flaunting in the eye of day,
Tremulous leaves with soft and silver lining,
    Buds that open only to decay;

7.

Brilliant hopes, all woven in gorgeous tissues,
    Flaunting gayly in the golden light;
Large desires with most uncertain issues,
    Tender wishes, blossoming at night.

8.

Everywhere about us they are glowing:
    Some, like stars, to tell us Spring is born;
Others, their blue eyes with tears o'erflowing,
    Stand like Ruth amid the golden corn.

#### 9.

Not alone in meadows and green alleys,
  On the mountain-top, and by the brink
Of sequestered pools in woodland valleys,
  Where the slaves of Nature stoop to drink;

#### 10.

Not alone in her vast dome of glory;
  Not on graves of bird and beast alone;
But in old cathedrals high and hoary,
  On the tombs of heroes carved in stone;

#### 11.

In the cottage of the rudest peasant;
  In ancestral homes, whose crumbling towers,
Speaking of the Past unto the Present,
  Tell us of the ancient games of flowers.

#### 12.

In all places, then, and in all seasons,
  Flowers expand their light and soul-like wings,
Teaching us, by most persuasive reasons,
  How akin they are to human things.

#### 13.

And with child-like, credulous affection,
  We behold their tender buds expand,—
Emblems of our own great resurrection,
  Emblems of the bright and better land.   *Longfellow.*

---

## No. 30.

### Our Country.

#### 1.

BRAVEST of nations, she moved through the shadow;
  Tempest and darkness encompassed her way;
Gleaming, she threaded the black thunder-billow;
And wreathed with the lightnings she rose into day.
  Bravest of nations!
Victory's palm on her white forehead lay.

2.

Grandest of nations, she stood in a halo, —
A glory that Justice and Liberty wrought;
Spirit-wings dripping from arches above her,
Auras of purified radiance brought.
  Grandest of nations!
Crowned with the light of her luminous thought.

3.

Fairest of nations! Love's beautiful lily
Oped on her bosom with honey to drip;
Weary ones yearned to her fragrance and whiteness,
 Thronging, the nectar of mercy to sip.
  Fairest of nations!
Deity's kiss upon forehead and lip.

4.

Strongest of nations! with white hands she lifted
Into the light the oppressed and the low;
Smote with her lightning the tyrant and traitor,
 Witnessing God to the world in the blow.
  Strongest of nations!
Angel avenging Humanity's woe.

5.

Swiftest of nations! pursuing with fleetness;
Sacred ideals thrown up from the soul;
On and yet onward with true poet-passion,
 Up where the mystical symphonies roll.
  Swiftest of nations!
Low are the stars from the infinite goal.

6.

Dearest of nations! Oh, pause not uncertain
 Of truest completeness! we tremble for thee:
Phantoms of terror brood over our gladness,
 All the world pants thy fruition to see.
  Dearest of nations!
Earth leans to Heaven with a passionate plea.

#### 7.

Light of the nations! bear onward the standard,
 Justice emblazoned and mercy empearled;
Not till the whole of the old wrong is righted,
 Let the wide folds of thy banner be furled.
  Light of the nations!
Star of humanity, hope of the world.
             *Augusta Cooper Bristol.*

## No. 31.

### On the Other Side.

#### 1.

WE go our way in life too much alone;
  We hold ourselves too much from all our kind;
Too often are we deaf to sigh and moan,
  Too often to the weak and helpless, blind;
Too often, where distress and want abide,
We turn, and pass upon the other side.

#### 2.

The other side is trodden smooth and worn
  By footsteps passing idly all the day:
Where lie the bruisèd ones who faint and mourn,
  Is seldom more than an untrodden way.
Our selfish hearts are for our feet a guide:
They lead us all upon the other side.

#### 3.

It should be ours the oil and wine to pour
  Into the bleeding wounds of stricken ones;
To take the smitten, and the sick and sore,
  And bear them where the stream of blessing runs.
Instead, we look about, the way is wide,
And so we pass by on the other side.

4.

O friends and brothers! gliding down the years,
Humanity is calling each and all
In tender accents, born of grief and tears:
God bids you listen to the thrilling call.
You cannot, in your cold and selfish pride,
Pass guiltless by upon the other side.   *L. B. Baker.*

## No. 32.
### Over There.

OH, the spacious, grand plantation,
    Over there!
Shining like a constellation,
    Over there!
Holy with a consecration,
From all tears and tribulation,
From all crime and grief and care,
To all uses good and fair,
    Over there!

Always brooding warm and golden,
Shines the mellow sunshine olden,
    Over there!
Never blighting shadow passes
On the silken, star-eyed grasses,
Waving wide their flowing hair
In the clear, translucent air,
    Over there!

Oh, the grand encamping mountains,
    Over there!
Oh, the sheeny, spouting fountains,
    Over there!
Oh, the boundless starlit arches,
Where the sun in glory marches,
On a road forever tending
Through bright legion worlds unending,
    Over there!

Brilliant blossoms breathe and burn,
    Over there!
Nectar drunken drops the fern
By the tulip's early urn,
    Over there!
Orange-buds and passion-flowers
Lattice sweet hymeneal bowers,
    Over there!

All the heavenly creatures born
Of the breeze, the dew, the morn,
In the divinest beauty grow,
Drape their purple, drift their snow,
Don their crimson, sheen their gold,
Shed their odors manifold
On the palpitating air,
On the flower-laden air,
    Over there!

Oh, the royal forests growing,
    Over there!
Breath of balsam ever flowing,
    Over there!
Pine trees sing their breezy chime,
Palm-trees lift their plumy prime
In the ever Eden time,
    Over there

And a passionate perfume
Fills the deep delicious gloom;
While through forest arcades ringing,
Lustrous birds are floating, singing,
    Over there

No salt tears the ground are drenching,
    Over there.
Faint with toil no thin forms blenching,
    Over there!
No more lifted hands outreaching
With a frantical beseeching;
No more desperate endeavors;
No more separating evers,
No more desolating nevers,
    Over there!

## No. 33.

### "The World would be the Better for it."

**1.**

IF men cared less for wealth and fame,
   And less for battle-fields and glory;
If, writ in human hearts, a name
   Seemed better than in song or story;
If men, instead of nursing pride,
   Would learn to hate it and abhor it;
     If more relied
       On love to guide. —
The world would be the better for it.

**2.**

If men dealt less in stocks and lands,
   And more in bonds and deeds fraternal;
If Love's work had more willing hands,
   To link this world with the supernal;
If men stored up Love's oil and wine,
   And on bruised human hearts would pour it;
     If "yours" and "mine"
       Would once combine, —
The world would be the better for it.

**3.**

If more would *act* the play of Life,
   And fewer spoil it in rehearsal;
If Bigotry would sheath its knife
   Till good became more universal;
If Custom, gray with ages grown,
   Had fewer blind men to adore it;
     If talent shone
       In truth alone, —
The world would be the better for it.

**4.**

If men were wise in little things,
   Affecting less in all their dealings;
If hearts had fewer rusted strings,
   To isolate their kindred feelings;
If men, when Wrong beats down the Right,
   Would strike together to restore it;
     If right made might
       In every fight, —
The world would be the better for it.

*M. H. Cobb.*

---

## No. 34.

### There Must be Something Wrong.

**1.**

WHEN earth produces, free and fair,
   The golden, waving corn;
When fragrant fruits perfume the air,
   And fleecy locks are shorn, —
While thousands move with aching head,
   And sing this ceaseless song, —
"We starve, we die oh! give us bread!"
   There must be something wrong.

**2.**

When wealth is wrought, as seasons roll,
   From off the fruitful soil;
When luxury from pole to pole
   Reaps fruit of human toil;
When, from a thousand, one alone
   In plenty rolls along,
While others only gnaw the bone, —
   There must be something wrong;

3.

And when production never ends,
 The earth is yielding ever;
A copious harvest oft begins,
 But distribution never;
When toiling millions work to fill
 The wealthy coffers strong;
When hands are crushed that work and till:
 There must be something wrong.

4.

When poor men's tables waste away
 To barrenness and drought,
There must be something in the way
 That's worth the finding out.

With surfeits one great table bends,
 While numbers move along;
While scarce a crust their board extends,—
 There must be something wrong.

5.

Then let the law give equal right
 To wealthy and to poor;
Let Freedom crush the arm of Might:
 We ask for nothing more.
Until this system is begun,
 The burden of our song
Must and can be this only one, —
 There must be something wrong.
*Eliza Cook.*

---

## No. 35.

### The World's Lie.

1.

I LOOKED from out the grating
 Of my spirit's dungeon-cell,
And I saw the life-tide rolling
 With a sullen, angry swell;
And the battle-ships were riding,
 Like leviathans in pride,
While their cannon-shot was raining
 On the stormy human tide.
Then my soul in anguish wept,
 Sending forth a wailing cry:
Said the World, "This comes from
  Heaven;"
 Said my Soul, "It is a LIE!"

2.

I looked from out the grating
 Of my spirit's dungeon-cell,
And I heard the solemn tolling
 Of a malefactor's knell.
And I saw a frowning gallows
 Reared aloft in awful gloom,
While a thousand eyes were glaring
 On a felon's horrid doom;
And a shout of cruel mirth
 On the wind was rushing by:
Said the World, "This comes from
  Heaven;"
 Said my Soul, "It is a LIE!"

3.

I looked from out the grating
 Of my spirit's dungeon-cell,
Where the harvest-wealth was blooming
 Over smiling plain and dell;
And I saw a million paupers
 With their foreheads in the dust;
And I saw a million workers
 Slay each other for a *crust!*
And I cried, "O God above me!
 Shall thy people always die?"
Said the World, "It comes from
  Heaven;"
 Said my Soul, "It is a LIE!"
*A. J. H. Duganne.*

## No. 36.
### The Inward Power.

WHEN the gloom is deepest round thee,
  When the bonds of grief have bound thee,
And, in loneliness and sorrow,
  By the poisoned springs of life
Thou sittest, yearning for a morrow
  That will free thee from the strife,
Look not upward, for above thee
  Neither sun nor star is gleaming;
Look not round for some to love thee,
  Put not faith in mortal seeming.
Lightly would they hold and leave thee;
E'en thy friends may all neglect thee;
But in the depths of thine own soul
Descend, and mightier powers unroll, —
Energies that long have slumbered
In its trackless depths unnumbered.
Speak the word! the power divinest
Will awake if thou inclinest.
Thou art loved in thine own kingdom:
  Rule thyself, thou rulest all.
Smile, when fortune's proud dominion
  Roughly touched shall rudely fall.
Be true unto thyself, and hear not
  Evil thoughts that would enslave thee:
God is in thee! Mortal, fear not:
  Trust in him and he will save thee.
          *From the German of Mahlmann.*

## No. 37.
### A Hymn of the Night.

#### 1.

IN the vast temple of the night
  I stand and muse with calm delight.
Its dome with silver flame is bright,
And drops of odorous, dewy light
    Fall from the urn-like moon.

The mountains that bear up the skies
Like shafts of sculptured emerald rise;
From the far North, in radiant guise,
Flame the ethereal mysteries,
    Robed in their crimson bloom.

### 2.

The leaves, the winds, the waters, flow
In blended cadence sweet and slow;
Now in great waves of song they go,
Then fall as dew-drops, faint and low,
    Drip from the myrtle-bough.
My spirit wakes in this great hour;
All holy things sweet influence shower;
The inward sight and sense and power
Unfoldeth like an opening flower:
    I rise transfigured now.

### 3.

Above me bends a vaster sky;
The storms, their wide wings beating, fly;
Dim shadows o'er the horizon lie;
And the eternal stars on high
    Shine through the NIGHT OF TIME.
All worn and scarred the toilers sleep;
Sad eyes in slumber weep and weep;
Strong souls their faithful vigil keep
Through the world's midnight dark and deep,
    With hope and love sublime.

### 4.

The outward night that round me lies
Must perish. Lo! the darkness dies;
Sweet voices in the brightening skies,
Sweet odors from the earth arise,
    Where flowers their bloom display.
The sun-burst with its golden wings
Has woke earth's blessed, beauteous things;
In silver robes the fountain springs;
All heaven with echoing music rings,
    To welcome in the DAY.

5.

*Thus*, waiting hearts, Time's storm-filled night,
Where Hate and Love, like gloom and light,
Have wrestled long in desperate fight,
Shall end. Rejoice! The True and Right
   To victory onward go.
No more dark fears the soul shall rend:
All hearts in Love's blest concord blend,
Bright seraphs to the earth descend,
Man dwell with God as friend with friend,
   And heaven fill all below.    *T. L. Harris.*

## No 38.

### Human Beauty.

AND is thy young eye dazzled with the pleasant form of beauty?
   This is but a lower love; still it hath its honor:
What God hath made, and meant to charm, let no man despise.
Nevertheless, as Reason's child, look thou wisely farther;
For age, disease, and care, and sin shall tarnish all the surface.
Reach a loftier love; be lured by the comeliness of mind, —
Gentle, kind, and calm or lustrous in the livery of knowledge.
And more, there is a higher grade. Force the mind to its perfection;
Win those golden trophies of consummate love.
Add unto the riches of the reason, and a beauty moulded to thy liking,
The precious things of nobler grace that well adorn a soul;
Thus be thou owner of a treasure, great in earth and heaven, —
Beauty, wisdom, goodness, in a creature like its God.

## No. 39.

### Revelations of the Divine.

1.

NOT in the thunder-peal that shakes the heaven,
   Not in the shoutings of the mighty sea,
Not where the fire-wave rolls from mountains riven,
   Not where the desolating whirlwinds flee;

Not where the crystal streamlets chime their stories,
    Not in the crash of elemental wars,
Not in the seasons with their changeful glories,
    Not in the skies with sun and moon and stars, —
Not there alone are heard the tones supernal
    Struck from the silence by Almighty Wings,
Not there alone resound the truths eternal
    Breathed from the Spirit of the King of kings.

### 2.

Though nature is a veil, of lightnings woven,
    Most beautiful and glorious to see,
And registers, in each progressive motion,
    The beatings of the heart of Deity;
Yet, through its folds, his loftiest revelations
    Of law and essence have been never made;
His voice, that awes and thrills the adoring nations,
    Comes not with sensual imagery arrayed.
It ripples, bathed in everlasting splendor,
    Through veins where Deity hath ever ran;
And speaks, in tones with Love's rich breathings tender,
    From the child-lips and heaven-bright soul of man.

### 3.

Not they who arrogate the name "Reformer,"
    Yet light God's altar with unhallowed fire;
Not they who stand like saints at every corner,
    Masking their lustful hearts in white attire;
Not they, who, thralled by sense, voluptuous breathings
    Call from the lyre as pours melodious wine;
Not they whose lips are curled with serpent wreathings,
    Who fetter with a creed the Love divine;
Not they who follow in the train of Fashion,
    And cringe to win the popular applause;
Not they enslaved to luxury or passion
    May teach mankind the everlasting laws.

### 4.

They who have borne the cross of scorn and sorrow,
    Enduring all with still forgiving love;
They who would nought from creeds of falsehood borrow,
    Waiting the revelation from above;

They who have faltered not when friend grew foeman,
  But trod through martyr-flames their fearless way;
They who have wavered not when rose-lipped woman
  Would lead them with her blandishments astray;
They who have ministered at Faith's pure altar,
  And in the robes of holiest virtue trod,—
They speak, in tones that vary not or falter,
  The truths of Heaven, the oracles of God.

### 5.

God speaketh in their lives of truth and beauty;
  God speaketh in their words of prophet fire;
God speaketh in their acts of loving duty,
  And noiseless charities that never tire.
And, haloed round with everlasting lustre,
  They shine transfigured in the might of soul;
And thronging generations round them cluster,
  To hear the music from their spirits roll.
For them earth shines more joyfully and fairer;
  Each word and deed of right lives on for aye;
Each heart-beat of their lives to man brings nearer
  The golden sunrise of the Eden day.  *T. L. Harris.*

---

## No. 40.

### Be Kind.

#### 1.

LET us be kind; for who has not
  Been more or less imperfect here?
Who would not have his sins forgot,
  Or blotted out by pity's tear?

#### 2.

Forgiveness is a gentle word,
  Upon whose tone how many live!

And, since we all have sinned or erred,
  Why not each other's faults forgive?

#### 3.

Oh! let our hearts be kindly cast,
  Until we cross the downward tide;
Like barks that feel a common blast,
  And come to anchor side by side.
        *C. D. Stuart.*

## No. 41.

### There's no Dearth of Kindness.

**1.**

THERE'S no dearth of kindness
   In this world of ours;
Only in our blindness
   We gather thorns for flowers.
Outward we are spurning,
   Trampling one another;
While we are inly yearning
   At the name of "Brother."

**2.**

There's no dearth of kindness
   Or love among mankind;
But, in darkling loneness,
   Hooded hearts grow blind.
Full of kindness tingling,
   Soul is shut from soul,
While they might be mingling
   In one kindred whole.

**3.**

As the wild rose bloweth,
   As runs the happy river,
Kindness freely floweth
   In the heart forever;
But if men will hanker
   Ever for golden dust,
Kingliest hearts will canker,
   Brightest spirits rust.

**4.**

There's no dearth of kindness
   In this world of ours;
Only in our blindness
   We gather thorns for flowers.
Oh! cherish God's best giving,
   Falling from above:
Life were not worth living,
   Were it not for love.

*Gerald Massey.*

---

## No. 42.

### The Island of Long Ago.

**1.**

OH! a wonderful stream is the river of Time,
   As it runs through the realms of years,
With a faultless rhythm and a musical rhyme,
And a broadening sweep and surge sublime,
   That blends with the ocean of tears.

**2.**

How the winters are drifting the flakes of snow,
   And the summers like buds between!
And the year in the sheaf, so they come and go
On the river's breast with its ebb and flow,
   As it glides through the shadow and sheen.

**3.**

There's a magical isle up the river of Time,
  Where the softest of airs are playing;
There's a cloudless sky and a tropical clime,
And a song as sweet as the vesper chime,
  And the Junes with the roses are staying.

**4.**

And the name of this isle is the Long Ago,
  And we bury our treasures there:
There are brows of beauty, and bosoms of snow;
There are heaps of dust — but we loved them so! —
  There are trinkets, and tresses of hair.

**5.**

There are fragments of songs that nobody sings,
  And a part of an infant's prayer;
There's a lute unswept, and a harp without strings;
There are broken vows, and pieces of rings,
  And the garments she used to wear.

**6.**

There are hands that waved when the fairy shore
  By the mirage is lifted in air;
And we sometimes hear through the turbulent roar
Sweet voices we heard in the days gone before,
  When the wind down the river was fair.

**7.**

Oh! remembered for aye be the blessed isle,
  All the days of life till night:
When the evening comes with its beautiful smile,
And our eyes are closing to slumber awhile,
  May that "island of soul" be in sight!     *B. F. Taylor.*

## No. 43.

### The Island of By and By.

**1.**

A POET sang to a thrilling harp
   Of the island of Long Ago;
And angels hearkened, and mortals wept,
   O'er the music's refluent flow:
Both spirits and mortals held their breath,
   The song was so sweet and low.

**2.**

O poet! singing your soul away,
   Your song is a sweet-breathed sigh;
But turn about while the finale flows
   From your fingers, and cast your eye
Adown Time's stream: there's an island
   there, —
   The island of By and By.

**3.**

When the clouds lift up on the foggy stream,
   And the atmosphere grows clear,
When we swiftly drift from the Long Ago,
   The emerald isle so dear,
It is sweet to know, that, as one land fades,
   The other is growing near.

**4.**

The Long Ago is the realm of forms
   Bitterly, bitterly dead;
The hand is ice with the broken ring,
   Marble the sacred head.
The harp is mist with the broken strings,
   Gone is the voice which led.

**5.**

The Long Ago is a burial-place,
   Marked by its marbles cold,
The bells which rock in the steeples gray
   Are ever solemnly tolled;
There Joy hangs off like a distant star,
   But Ruin and Change are bold.

**6.**

But By and By is the realm of souls,
   The region of fadeless blooms:
Upon the rim of its vernal shores
   Never a breaker booms;
And never a storm-cloud in the sky,
   Pitted with darkness, looms.

**7.**

When the clouds lift up and the wind is fair,
   Look out with your soul, and see
The silvery foliage wave and flash
   High up in the sapphire sea:
Each leaflet speaking as 'twere a tongue,
   "Here is immortality."

**8.**

You will see, maybe, in the melting air,
   The flutter of drapery,
And Eden's blossoms flashing in hair
   Rippling all goldenly;
And smiling lips which will never pale,
   Wailing, oh! rosily.

**9.**

O Poet! you with a ring of flame
   Burning about your brow,
Throw all the fire of your passionate heart
   Into a new song now:
Sing of the island of By and By,
   While angels and mortals bow.
                  *Emma Tuttle.*

## No. 44.
### God is Forever with Man.

**1.**

SING, little bluebird, the message ye bring, —
    God is forever with man!
Cleave the soft air with a rapturous wing, —
    God is forever with man!
Warble the story to forest and rill,
Sweep up the valley, and bear to the hill
The sacred refrain of your passionate trill, —
    God is forever with man!

**2.**

Open, bright roses, and blossom the thought,
    God is forever with man!
Precious the meaning your beauty hath wrought,
    God is forever with man!
Spread out the sweet revelation of bloom,
Lift and release from an odorous tomb
The secret embalmed in a humid perfume, —
    God is forever with man!

**3.**

Dance, happy billows, and say to the shore,
    God is forever with man!
Echo, sea-caverns, the truth evermore,
    God is forever with man!
Bear on, creation, the symbol and sign
That being unfolds in an aura divine,
And soul moveth on in an infinite line:
    God is forever with man!

*Augusta Cooper Bristol.*

# CONSTITUTION.

PREAMBLE. — For intellectual and moral progress, and the social improvement of our children and ourselves, we organize under the name of THE PROGRESSIVE LYCEUM, and adopt the following Constitution: —

### ART. I. — MEMBERSHIP.

Any person can become a member of this Association by subscribing his or her name to this Constitution.

### ART. II. — OFFICERS.

The officers shall consist of a Conductor, a Guardian of Groups, a Watchman, a Librarian, a Treasurer, a Secretary, a Musical Director, three Guards, and a corps of Leaders. All offices may be filled by either sex.

### ART. III. — OFFICERS. — HOW ELECTED.

All officers shall be elected by a majority of votes, cast by ballot by the members of the Lyceum. The Conductor shall announce, the two Lyceum Sessions immediately preceding that on which his term of office expires, that on that day re-election of officers will take place.

### ART. IV. — DUTIES OF OFFICERS.

SECTION 1. The Conductor shall act as the presiding officer. His duties during the Lyceum Session shall be to announce the order of exercises, superintend the recitations, lead in the Calisthenic exercises, and otherwise perform such duties as his office involves.

SECT. 2. The duty of the Guardian of Groups shall be to superintend the several groups during the Lyceum sessions; distribute the badges; lead the responses in the recitations; lead in the march, bearing the Guardian's banner; and to keep a journal of the names of members, and of the sessions.

SECT. 3. The duties of the Watchman shall be to keep every thing in order. He is, as his name indicates, a watcher, constantly on the alert, caring for all the details of the session.

SECT. 4. The duty of the Librarian shall be to take charge of the books, papers, and other business connected therewith, for the Lyceum.

SECT. 5. The duty of the Treasurer shall be to receive and account for all moneys of the Lyceum, from whatever source received, and pay to the orders of the Secretary, countersigned by the Conductor. He shall make a quarterly report to the Conductor.

SECT. 6. The duty of the Secretary shall be to make a record of all meetings of the Lyceum, all business transacted, and attend to its correspondence.

SECT. 7. The duty of the Musical Director shall be to take charge of the musical requirements of the Lyceum, and lead the musical exercises of its sessions.

SECT. 8. The Guards shall take charge of the hall and ante-rooms; extend civilities to visitors; prepare the banners for the marches; arrange the seats, and otherwise assist, as the Conductor may require.

SECT. 9. The Leaders shall be the instructors of their respective Groups; keep group-books, and aim to be evangels of love and truth to the minds under their care.

### ART. V.— THE EXECUTIVE BOARD.

The Conductor, Guardian, and Librarian constitute an Executive Board, having in charge the property of the Lyceum. These, with all the other officers, constitute a Board of Managers.

### ART. VI.— SUSPENSIONS AND EXPULSIONS.

No amendment or law shall ever be passed, affecting the religious opinions or social standing of any officer or member; and no officer or member shall be expelled or suspended, except for insubordination or neglect of duty.

### ART. VII.— VACANCIES.

Shall be filled *pro tem.* by the Conductor; permanent vacancies shall be announced to the Lyceum by the Conductor, and new officers elected to the positions in the same manner as at the general election.

### ART. VIII.— AMENDMENTS.

This Constitution may be changed or amended by presenting the proposed change or amendment in writing at a session of the Lyceum; at the second session thereafter it shall be acted on; and, if it receive a two-thirds majority of the votes of all members taken by ballot, it shall be adopted.

## GENERAL BY-LAWS.

ARTICLE 1. The officers of this Society shall be elected annually, on the day the incumbent's term of office expires.

ART. 2. The officers of the Lyceum shall meet for the transaction of business pertaining to the Lyceum, at least once a month. The Conductor can call such a meeting whenever he thinks desirable.

ART. 3. At such meetings it shall be lawful, whenever a majority of officers are present, to appoint a Secretary, pass by-laws, and transact all business connected with the Lyceum. The proceedings, however, must be submitted to the next session of the Lyceum, and cannot be adopted except by a majority vote of members.

ART. 4. Such system of finance may be adopted as receives the approval of a majority of the members.

ART. 5. The Conductor, Guardian, Librarian, and Musical Director can choose their own assistants.

# THE PHILOSOPHY AND LANGUAGE OF COLORS.

LIGHT, in its absolute sense, is the consciousness of truth. In its restricted sense, it is a force revealing material objects to the vision by color, and by contrast of light with shade. Our principal light is from the sun, and is transmitted to us in rays which traverse interstellar space, moving with a velocity of one hundred and ninety-two thousand miles per second; and, notwithstanding its direction is straight from the point of emission, its forward motion is by waves or undulations. Light is radiant *power*, luminous in character, and really the impulse to motion. It is transmitted by ethereal undulations, as sound is by those of the atmosphere, with only this difference: that, while the air-particles move back and forth in the same direction as the advancing wave, — "normal vibrations;" the ethereal particles move across, — "transverse vibrations." This corresponds with the location and anatomical structure of the ear and eye.

The rays of light, in passing from a rarer to a denser medium, are refracted and turned from their original course; and, according to the refrangibility, is shown the degree of resistance manifested by opposing forces, the intensity of undulations, and the kind of color; and in these colors are realized in positive, utilized effects, the radiant forces of nature. It is found that thirty-nine thousand waves or undulations of red light would measure an inch, while fifty-seven thousand five hundred are required of violet light to fill the same space. The intermediate colors increase in their number of waves from red to violet.

As light moves one hundred and ninety-two thousand miles per second, that length of ray streams into the eye each second. Reduce this distance to inches, and multiply the sum by thirty-nine thousand, — the product will be the number of waves of red light beating upon the retina of the eye each second. Multiply the same number by fifty-seven thousand five hundred, and it will give the number of waves per second affecting the eye when looking at violet. Therefore, the colored light depends upon the length of the ethereal wave, as the pitch of sound depends upon the length of the air-wave. The degree and intensity with which the ethereal waves beat upon the retina, is the cause of the consciousness of color.

In the solar spectrum are the radiant forces of the Universe expressed in miniature scale. A beam of light passing through a prism is bent, divided, and spread out, displaying seven colors successively, called the solar spectrum. Each color shows the refraction of its cause to be at a different angle. The last refracted ray is Red; the next Orange; then Yellow, Green, Blue, Indigo, and Violet; the last named has the highest refraction. Three of these colors, viz., Yellow, Red, and Blue, are called the Primaries, from which all the other colors are compounded. Corresponding with these three Primaries are developed three characteristic forces called "radiant forces," of which all others in nature are but modifications.

The characteristic power of Yellow is illumination; revealing through the eye things of nature by relief from darkness. Prof. Draper has proven that the changes in the vegetable kingdom are due to the force in this color and its compounds, — orange and green. It seems to be the *illuminating* and *directing agent* of the other forces.

Red is the ray developing heat : it acts to separate and force apart. Blue is the chemical ray : its function is to combine.

The motion by which each force is known and measured is convertible from one form to another. Consequently, those undulations of light which flow at the rate of thirty-nine thousand in an inch, and exciting a consciousness of Red, will, when converted by increasing the number to flow at the rate of about forty-five thousand five hundred in the same space, develop a new force, and excite the consciousness of a new color, — Yellow. With waves intensified to about fifty-two thousand five hundred, measuring the same, Blue, the third Primary, is revealed, developing a third force. Between these Primaries are their compounds, — Orange, Green, and Purple (Secondaries), partaking the character of their components.

In the difference between these two sums of the chromatic extremes of the spectrum, and the achromatic white and black, consists the field or scope of vision; beyond these, the waves are either too slow or pitched too high to affect the optic nerve. And yet all in darkness exists an infinite vital but unseen Energy, which has dispersed beauty and the forces of execution in a single ray of light.

Light emitted by the sun, and entering our atmosphere, becomes refracted and dispersed when this trio of energies are unfolded, exerting a three-fold influence over matter as displayed in the economy of our world. By the solar ray the mineral world is raised to the organized condition; vegetation springs into existence, upon which the animal world subsists; heat rarifies the air unequally; winds in currents flow, and vapory storm-clouds sweep o'er the earth, and fall in refreshing rain. This, absorbed by the ground, nourishes vegetation, gathers into fountains, channels the earth with streams, and turns the sluggish mill-wheel of industry, the whole earth is vivified, and beauty rises from desolation. Flowers cover the landscape, rainbows span the heavens, daylight follows darkness, and season succeeds to season. The full harvest of a golden summer is prepared through the crystal medium of frozen earth, by this magazine of supernal force, — "the Sun of Light." " And instead," says Prof. Youmans, "of a dead material world, we have a living organism of Spiritual Energies."

Now, are all these things without meaning in God's economy? It cannot be. By them we live and have our consciousness; and in the proper use and appreciation of them by our faculties, our lives grow harmonious, peaceful, and happy. Therefore there must be meaning, and consequently purpose; if purpose, an intelligent motor power, — God, or a Divine consciousness underlying all these forces.

## THE LANGUAGE OF COLORS.

These phenomena possess utility and significance, corresponding with the forces revealed in the colors of the solar spectrum. If the force revealed in red is expansion by repulsion, its significance is individualizing by separating *selfish* and *discordant;* if in blue it is chemical combination, its significance is attraction by affinity, — combining; if in yellow it is chromatic intensity, — power of impressing, — its significance is light from comprehension and understanding.

Again, corresponding with the Primaries is the significance of purpose in Yellow; plan in Blue; means or modes in Red, as follows: the divine purpose is happiness for man; the Divine plan to accomplish this is character; and the means for the execution of the plan is experience.

It is plain that power, which exists in nature as an executive agent of intelligence, must have an existence also in the intelligent human mind, and is the impulse of vital force to motion. Hence those motions which are consonant between nature's impartation or reflection, and the human receptivity or inner consciousness, constitutes the means of sensuous perception, which is the basis of experimental knowledge. And this power, manifested in motion, corresponds with laws governing mind in the application of its experience, — the basis of character. Intelligence and significance in nature evidently harmonizes with intelligence and significance in ourselves; proving our unity with the divine in character, — consequently in the sources of angelic happiness.

The perceptions of the mind may be classified as Sensuous, Intellectual, and Spiritual. These may be subdivided indefinitely, blending with and neutralizing each other. As represented by colors, they correspond with the radiant forces; and as the forces are commutable only by motion, so are these colors and their significance neutralized and subordinated by each other. If in Yellow we have brightness and spirituality as its significance; in Blue intellectual combination, — unity; in Red, sensuous appreciation, — repulsiveness, then, by blending any two of these colors and their attributes, we will get an intermediate quality of color and character corresponding with the wants of that nature, generating the energies to be united. Thus spiritual perception and energy, blending or acting together with sensuous perception and its energy, will produce, as a dominant trait, *will-power*. Heat, we know, transmits an expansive energy, overcomes the force of cohesion, and, with increased temperature, repulsion will predominate, when matter becomes fugitive, thrown from communities into individual bodies. Hence, this force in character is contrifugal; but the spiritual acts with this force. Repulsion consequently has its purpose, which is to embody spirit in finite conceptions; and that spirit is to grow to an individual character by overcoming and controlling inferior forces; it must struggle over life's outward flowing tide to the centre of conscious divine unity; which struggle necessitates *will-power*.

If we compound Red and Blue, the effect will be Purple; of the significance, Blue is intellectual, combining, and constructing; it is a cold, calculating agent, and, like its correspondent chemical force, will, when prompted, disorganize to form new combinations. The character developed by these two energies will be, — ambition, co-operative energy, and concentration of power. This temperament is instinctive and aggrandizing. Chemically, substances combine the best that are the most antagonistical: indifferently in the dark, better in diffused daylight; but, in a beam of sunlight, the combination is perfect. Therefore, when the attributes of Red and Blue are brought under the influence of, and guided by, spirituality, we have chemically a new compound, which, morally speaking, develops a superior character. When spiritually enlightened, we sacrifice sensuous desires from a consciousness of duty, which lifts us into heavenly union. Thus the sensuous is transformed into a spiritual life. Combine Yellow — signifying light, spirituality — with Blue (blue is intellectual), we have Green as a color, and harmony as its significance; which must result from the two energies acting together. A harmonious mind combines and classifies for the sake of principles; this temperament is intuitive. In the consciousness of harmony, there is rest. Its beautiful correspondent in the material world is Green, — the subduing and harmonizing garment of earth; the connecting link between the colors Red, Orange, and Yellow, on the side of light; and Blue, Indigo, and Violet, on the side of shade.

We have seen the qualities of character symbolized by the Primaries; and also more specific qualities by the Secondaries. There are also Tertiaries compounded by Secondaries possessing their significance, approaching the neutrals, — as Orange and Green produce Citrine (on the side of light), in which Yellow predominates as two, to one of Blue, and one of Red. Its location is among the qualities of spirituality blending with intellect; its significance, Truthfulness, Fidelity.

Olive, compounded of Purple and Green, Blue predominating (and on the side of shade), is a Neutral, constructive in character. Significance, — cold, cautious, and artful.

Russet, compounded of Purple and Orange, Red predominating, approaches a Neutral on the side of shade; and is within the sphere of Repulsiveness. Significance, — Self-reliance. Neutral Black is formed by compounding the Primaries in pigments of a low but pure grade, according to their combining equivalents, — as Yellow, three parts; Red, five; and Blue, eight. The significance of this Neutral (Black) being the absorbent of heat, — selfish repulsiveness; is an active degradation both in color and character, — society's scapegoat.

The following colors will subordinate each other by *contrast*, according to their combining numbers; that is, their wave-motions, impinging upon the retina, will neutralize each other into harmony: —

3 Yellow, with 13 Purple.  13 Purple, with 27 Citrine.
8 Blue,   "   8 Orange.    8 Orange,  "  24 Olive.
5 Red,    "  11 Green.    11 Green,   "  27 Russet.

But the harmony in Nature is principally accomplished not by *contrast*, but by *analogy*; i.e., those colors that are similar to each other are placed side by side, as in the rainbow.

Gray, as a color, is a mixture of White with Black; but Gray, as an effect upon the eye, produced by harmonious combination of pure tints subordinating each other *en masse*, should be denominated "Blonde;" for this is the fair and translucent human complexion. This effect of Gray Blonde is the *expression* of character, as Gray upon the other extreme represents the *absence* of character. From the gray rocks in the early ages of our earth, by commutation through attrition, has this effect (Blonde) been moulded to represent and express the intelligence in the "human face" by birthright "Divine."

White, added to any of these Primaries, Secondaries, and Tertiaries, produces innumerable colors, hues, and tints. For instance: a reddish purple broken by white, yields a Pearl; if white predominates, a Lilac. Add white to red, we get Rose-color and Pink; and so with all other colors indefinitely. White harmonizes with all colors; likewise the grays and blondes.

When an infant soul from the shores of the Infinite unseen has drifted in its bark to this terrestrial world, here to develop its energies and life's most hidden meaning, it is compelled to struggle against adversities, and buffet the tide of circumstances; to reach at last some quiet haven hewn from its own celestial nature, there to repose in the glorious sunbeams of a conscious unity with its God. To accomplish this, circumstances compel it to care for itself; the mind, therefore, accepts the quickest and surest method. If we are burned by fire, we determine, then, our proper relation to it; if nipped by frost, we avoid those temperatures in the future; if diseased by indulgence, watchfulness is established. Thus, by experience through temptation, do we learn the laws of life.

Human life, in its beginning and progress, as represented by colors and their significance with their neutrals, unfolds in character as follows:—

*Gray.* — Mind is without any distinguishable character, — Innocence.

*Lilac and Pearl.* — The first flush of aurora; objects are sensed in the dim, mental haze of uncertainty, — Trusting, Unsuspecting.

*Pink and Rose.* — The rising mental light defines the world with a silvery edge of beauty, but stripes the earth with shadows dark and foreboding, — Modesty, Diffidence.

*Red and Crimson.* — The mind is absorbed in a sensuous life, — Ardor, Zeal.

*Russet and Maroon, or Wine Color.* — Active and self-reliant, — Power and Ambition.

*Purple and Violet.* — When the spirit shall see that power and ambition are all vanity and vexation, and strive for a better life, the result must be, — Aspiration.

*Blue and Indigo.* — When love shall do for love's sake, — Combining, Unity.

*Green and Citrine.* — Unity is accomplished in the harmonious connections of the lower with the higher attributes. In music, the bass with the treble; the colors of the light with the shaded side of the spectrum; the reds and yellows of earth with the blue of heaven. A mind that can view things terrestrial and celestial from this central point, rests in, — Harmony.

*Emerald and Light Olive.* — Faith in the power of truth, — Truthfulness, Fidelity.

*Orange and Dark Orange.* — The channel of energy, — Endurance, Perseverance, Will.

*White and Blue-White.* — Characteristic expression of purity through victorious struggling, — Purity.

*Yellow and Gold.* — The spirit "born into the glorious liberty of the sons of God." This is the golden radiated halo of archangels and is, — Inspirational.

Thus grows the spirit by degrees, led outward and upward in responsibility from the first emotional consciousness and inexperienced innocence, as symbolized in Gray, to the deepest sensuous appreciation, symbolized in earth's positive color, Red. From this experimental knowledge does the combining force of mind mould the character, by restraint and by aspiration, as symbolized in Blue and its compounds. Then, streaming downward at first in soft, pathetic rays, kindles in the soul a celestial fire that glows with inexpressible beauty, consumes all discord, and converts all emotions of vital force into vibrations of one synthetical harmony of adjustment in philosophy, as in Green. Then onward still, where the recipient weaves from the radiating threads of God's garment of purest white, — "vesture of angels, — fabrics of virtue to clothe the imprisoned soul; and, last of all, in the grandest attributes given by an Infinite Parent to a finite child who grasps and executes the divine economy, by direct volition, combining star with star, atom with atom, and soul with soul, by this all-powerful agent and redeemer, a beam of light, — as in Yellow.

Hence it is plain, that colors are God's language, and speak with a force not to be misunderstood, if man will but unstop his ears and hear, or open his eyes, and see; for it is self-evident there *is a purpose:* then there must follow a *plan* upon which to execute it, and the *means* wherewith it shall be executed. This purpose is *happiness;* the plan is *character;* and the means *experience.* While experience is the scaffolding over which we build the arch, virtue must be the material of construction; and conscience — light, or the knowledge of right from wrong — is the keystone of union.

On the following page the Colors, their language, groups, duplicate groups, and numbers, are arranged in tabular form. The long, vertical bracket, embracing the whole table, signifies the beginning of life and its ultimation in perfected character, attained by a pilgrimage in *experience* of the radiant forces by the faculties inherent in man, and which are classified as attributes corresponding with the forces developed by the three primary colors on the left-hand side of the page, and included within smaller brackets. These attributes, blending with each other as do the colors, produce characteristic sentiments corresponding with the color standing opposite to it; and these columns of colors, sentiments, groups, and numbers (their duplicates being of equal value), are interlaced, making it easy to distinguish what colors, &c., are for the first series in the Lyceum, and which for the duplicates.

## SCALE OF COLORS, WITH THEIR CORRESPONDING GROUPS.

| ATTRIBUTES. | COLORS | and their LANGUAGE. | GROUPS. | NOS. | AGE OF MEMB'RS. |
|---|---|---|---|---|---|
| NEUTRAL,—without character, and subordinating the | Light Gray | Innocence | Fountain | 1 | 6 years and under |
| | Gray | Germs of Hope | Aurora | 13 | |
| | Lilac | Trusting | Stream | 2 | 7 years |
| | Pearl | Unsuspecting | Sunbeam | 14 | 7 " |
| | Pink | Modesty | River | 3 | 8 " |
| | Rose | Diffidence | Lawn | 15 | 8 " |
| Influence of RED, which is physical energy and sensuous experience, reaching into the | Red | Ardor | Lake | 4 | 9 " |
| | Crimson | Zeal | Grotto | 16 | 9 " |
| | Russet | Pride | Sea | 5 | 10 " |
| | Maroon | Self-Reliance | Glen | 17 | 10 " |
| | Purple | Restraint | Ocean | 6 | 11 " |
| | Violet | Aspiration | Sylvan | 18 | 11 " |
| Influence of BLUE, —intellectual and mental energies combining by affinity; and blending with the influ- | Blue | Combining Power | Shore | 7 | 12 " |
| | Indigo | Love of Unity | Valley | 19 | 12 " |
| | Green | Harmony | Banner | 8 | 13 " |
| | Citrine | Concord | Floral | 20 | 13 " |
| | Emerald | Truthfulness | Star | 9 | 14 " |
| | Light Olive | Fidelity | Garland | 21 | 14 " |
| ence of YELLOW, —the inspiring energy of light and spirituality; producing a perfect character, — the arch-angelic. | Orange | Will | Excelsior | 10 | 15 " |
| | Light Orange | Firmness | Mountain | 22 | 15 " |
| | White | Purity | Liberty | 11 | 16 and 17 yrs. |
| | Yellow White | Chastity | Temple | 23 | 16 and 17 yrs. |
| | Yellow | Inspiration | Summer | 12 | 18 years and upwards |
| | or Gold | Spirituality | Evangel | 24 | |

## GROUPS.

WHERE there is one instructor to lead, and one pupil to learn, the union is an incipient Lyceum. We recommend that Groups be formed, without respect to numbers, just as fast as additions and qualifications may warrant, and no faster. Nor should children of the same grade be separated to form a second Lyceum in the same hall. When necessary, Groups can be duplicated, under the management of one Leader, the standards — "Fountain" and "Aurora," for instance — erected over the seats. Twelve Groups are a complete Lyceum. An excess, or duplicates, are indications of superior progress and success. We have made but slight changes in the titles or arrangements of the Groups, regarding, as we do, the Group system projected by Mr. Davis as both beautiful and natural.

Suppose there is need of a new Group in a Lyceum, not included in our series. Of course it should harmonize in color and sentiment with the rest: let the Leader carefully inspect the Scale herein defined and classified, and use the color, ratio, or data, choosing such colors and their subordinates as the new title of the Group and its correlative sentiment may demand. Thus we can have any number of additional Groups, all matching together in the sacred orders of spiritual science.

---

## GROUP STANDARDS.

THE more we study the forces of nature, the more intimate do we feel with God, nestling, child-like, in the bosom of the Divine; but these spiritual communings, so full of joy, are simply the result of the subordination of nature's forces in us, under intelligent control. Hence, beauty of character is not eccentricity, but subordination — balance of faculties. All our symbols should correspond with the principle on which the mind is organized — unity in diversity; that the spirit may be invited out by scenes of variety and harmony in combination. Color pleases us most when subordinated by complementary colors. Constructing upon this law, we have STANDARDS for the Groups to rally around — not Targets; and heraldic shields instead of ellipses, representing by colors the character of the Groups.

The staff should be constructed of light, durable wood, from six to seven feet long, three-fourths of an inch thick, projecting eight or ten inches above the Shield, terminating with a walnut ball. The shield is supported at the top by an arm at right angles with the staff, extending two inches on each side beyond the shield, having walnut balls upon the ends.

On the front, at the top of the SHIELD, light-gray colored silk is used for all the Standards except Fountain Group, where *white* should be used, the gray of the shield being the sentiment color, on which the name of the Group is put in gilt letters (of gilt paper). The centre color below is the one for sentiment: the color surrounding

## THE LANGUAGE OF COLORS.

it is the one which subordinates or complements it, and should, as near as possible, be combined according to their numbers, if contrasted; but if by analogy, arrange to suit taste. Then bind it with a silk cord, nearly a quarter-inch in width, of a steel-gray color, and from the nicks of the arms near the balls, let the cord swing half-way down the shield upon the back, and upon the staff, at the top of the shield, tack the cord in three loops; then swing round to arms again, as seen in the drawing. The sentiment color covers the whole of the back, upon which is placed the number of Group, and, if you choose, the language of the color.

Board with Wire Loops.

Front of Standard.      Back of Standard.

Cut the shield from *card-board;* then fasten it by a few small tacks, driven through against a flat-iron, so they will clinch without breaking, to a thin strip of board, to which you must have already glued the balls. The paper and wood boards are fastened together at the centre; where the staff rises put two wire loops through the boards about half an inch from the top. Be sure to have the ends clinched in the boards, so they may not loosen, and wear the silk. Have these wire loops lean towards each other, extending scarcely above the top of the shield, and be about three-fourths of an inch apart. With these loops suspend the shield to the staff by two very small screw-eyes, correspondingly spaced on the staff; a little opening is filed in the eye at the stem to admit the wire loop; then the standard can swing or be fastened by a ribbon at the bottom of the staff.

After sewing the gray piece of silk (it should be about five inches wide) to the sentiment color, double it, lay the shield upon it, and mark with a pencil; be sure not to get the silk too small, so as to warp the card-board, nor yet too large, or it will appear baggy and slovenly made. Before inserting the board in its silk covering, sew on the complementary color, as seen in the drawing. Paste white paper over the board to cover the tack-heads or any dark spots. You will find the lower part of the shield too large to pass the narrow part of the silk sack: to avoid any strain, press with the fingers the two edges of the shield, making the large part concave, while another slips the sack on; then sew up the top, and bind it with cord, tacking tightly around the wire loops, leaving them projecting above.

The pattern for the Shield is about the width of dress silk, cutting to good advantage, adjusted to be a little longer than wide. The cord used for binding should be deeper gray than the silk upon which the letters are placed, and the tassels the same shade. This harmonizes with all the other colors.

It will require but a few evenings for the Leaders to construct the standards. Their brilliant effect in the Lyceum will amply repay for all the labor and cost.

"A thing of beauty is a joy forever."

## BANNERS AND BADGES.

AFTER adopting the sentiment colors we have given for the respective Standards, the same color, of different or like intensity, will be proper for Banners and Badges. We give engravings of a set of banners, with emblematic mottoes, which we do not hesitate to offer for your consideration, although their immediate adoption by Lyceums already organized may not be deemed expedient. The American flag is recommended by Mr. Davis, and is at present used in nearly all Lyceums. It is a beautiful banner, and is dear to the heart of every citizen of the Republic; but a national flag to us seems not in keeping with the spirit of the Lyceum movement. Where, however, Lyceums are already supplied, we do not wish to urge a change as essential to progress, but simply offer you our best and most inspirational designs.

Across the blue ground of the banner is the "Bow in the Clouds," emblematic of "Good Will," — the actual presence of light. A gilt sun on the shoulders of the cross-arms of the standard, with a gilt ball, and dove holding an olive-branch in its beak, surmounting the whole; festoons of green drapery in front, and magenta behind; tassels and binding to correspond. If preferred, in place of the Bow, put "PROGRESSIVE LYCEUM," on a blue ground, in gilt letters. This banner may be placed on the

Conductor's stand during sessions, facing the school. It is beautiful to be borne in the front on festive occasions.

THE LYCEUM BANNER.

THE GUARDIAN'S BANNER.

This is of a light creamy color, or yellowish white, with deep purple fringe as border, and tassels depending from the gilt ball at the extremity of the staff.

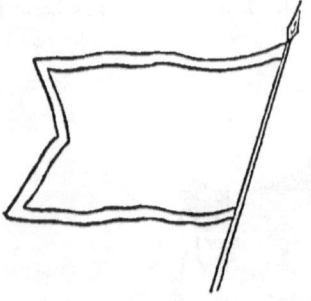

**FOUNTAIN GROUP.**
COLORS. — Light gray, with scarlet border.
SENTIMENT. — Innocence.

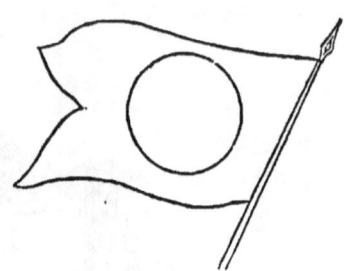

**LAKE GROUP.**
COLORS. — Red, blue within the circle.
SENTIMENT. — Ardor.

**STREAM GROUP.**
COLORS. — Lilac ground, with white crescent.
SENTIMENT. — Trustfulness.

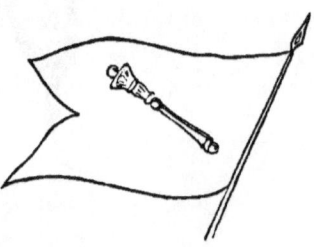

**SEA GROUP.**
COLORS. — Russet ground, the sceptre gilt or yellow.
SENTIMENT. — Authority.

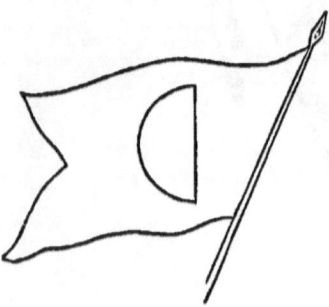

**RIVER GROUP.**
COLORS. — Pink ground, the half-orb lilac or pearl.
SENTIMENT. — Modesty.

**OCEAN GROUP.**
COLORS. — Purple ground, the anchor white.
SENTIMENT. — Aspiration.

## BANNERS AND BADGES. 147

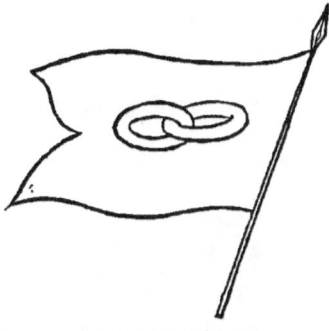

SHORE GROUP.
COLORS. — Blue ground, the links brown.
SENTIMENT. — Unity.

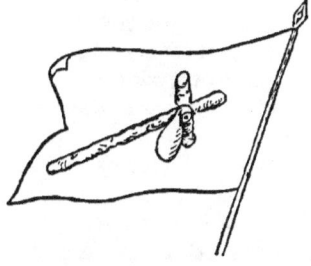

EXCELSIOR GROUP.
COLORS. — Light orange, the cross in deep orange.
SENTIMENT. — Will.

BANNER GROUP.
COLORS. — Green ground, the harp light brown.
SENTIMENT. — Harmony.

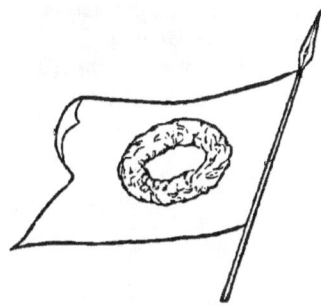

LIBERTY GROUP.
COLORS. — White ground, the wreath gilt.
SENTIMENT. — Purity.

STAR GROUP.
COLORS. — Emerald green, shield in red, white, and blue.
SENTIMENT. — Truthfulness.

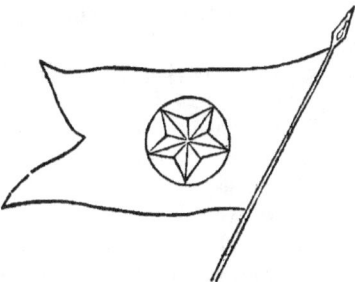

SUMMER GROUP.
COLORS. — Yellow, the star silver or pearl, on a white ground.
SENTIMENT. — Inspiration.

If preferable, or more convenient, plain banners of the sentiment color may be used, with a single contrasting border, varied at pleasure.

## BADGES.

CONDUCTOR'S BADGE. — A gold or gilt Sun, surrounded by a silver circle touching the longest rays; velvet ribbons, green and red, — dark, rich shades.

GUARDIAN'S BADGE. — A silver or pearl five-rayed Star, in the centre of a blue velvet or silk rosette, with two streamers.

MUSICAL DIRECTOR'S BADGE. — A Harp, from under which fall green velvet streamers.

GUARD'S AND WATCHMAN'S BADGE. — An Eagle holding a sceptre suspended by a chain in his beak; ribbons brown, — russet.

LIBRARIAN'S BADGE. — A silver book; buff and pink ribbons.

SECRETARY'S BADGE. — A gold book, with emerald ribbons.

TREASURER'S BADGE. — Two gold links depending from a bar; white ribbon streamers.

LEADER'S BADGE. — A silver shield, the sentiment of which is "Truth, the protector," from which depend two streamers of the sentiment color of the respective Group standards.

The badges for Group members may be the same as their Leader's, or simply a ribbon rosette of the Group.

The badges are worn on the left breast. Each Group should have a box for them so they will not become disordered. The box should be of the Group color.

---

## *PESTALOZZIAN MAXIMS.*

1. Let the child be trained to feel that the aim of his existence is higher than his existence.

2. To become capable of educating a child, the teacher must himself become a little child.

3. It is not by forcing the child's nature into the form of your own nature, but by giving yourself up to the nature of the child, that you can return to childlike simplicity.

4. Never behave *childish* to a child, but teach him with a childlike heart.

5. Do not strive to hide your imperfections from the child, but rather strive to avoid their influencing your conduct; and, when you have done this, avow them fully. But, to be able to avow them without impairing your influence, you must get rid of all those imperfections which you cannot avow without losing your dignity in the child's eyes.

6. Never let your pupils look up to you for the *ground of their conviction*, but let them find the proof of their knowledge in their understanding.

## MORAL LESSONS.

THE Lyceum is designed to cultivate our moral and intellectual being, to the end that perfect harmony of life may be the result of the supremacy of our spiritual natures.

We should, therefore, select such themes from the vast encyclopædia of thought as will directly contribute to this result. If we, as instructors, are truly enlightened in love of truth, we shall find a divinity in every thing we touch. The simplest language which clearly expresses the idea we wish to convey is the best. If we employ the simple, yet expressive, words of children, use illustrations which they can comprehend, become their companions and fellow-students, irradiating warmth from enthusiastic hearts, we are sure of success.

To create interest, and carry conviction, we must *feel* what we say. If we would impress a great moral truth, it must come from a soul of which it is a part; falling from the lips like a jet of water from a sunlit fountain, carrying with it the demonstration of its worth and beauty in the noble life which it helps to illuminate. Such are true teachers. Under their instructions, the mind of the child will expand to wisdom and harmony as naturally as the roses unfold in the sunshine of June. To make our lives worthy of imitation by those we teach should be the ceaseless effort of all who lead the young.

Feel what you impart, and the attentive mind will almost catch your thought before it is uttered in words, so strong is the silent influence which we exert upon other minds.

By employing objects as illustrations, in giving such instructions as would render it desirable, the keenest interest is at once awakened, and the child not only understands what is said, but retains it more easily for future use. The following is suggestive of subjects which may be introduced :

## GENERAL SUBJECTS.

GEOLOGY, Chemistry, Physiology, Philosophy, Psychology, History — Effects of climate on national and individual character — Influence of art and science — Civilization — Peace — Degrees of love and wisdom — Best methods of diffusing knowledge and truth — Prophecy — Intuition — Instinct — Reason — Human consciousness — Inspiration — Revelation — Mediumship : its uses and abuses — Prayer — Spirit — The spirit world — God — Marriage — The virtues — The vices — Evil Spirits — Death — Religion — The ministry of angels — Wisdom — Truth — Immortality.

## INDIVIDUAL DEVELOPMENT.

A DISTINGUISHING feature of the Lyceum should be the practical unfolding of the leading genius of the pupil. The attempt to mould Nature diverse from her inclinations, or to force a child to think and feel like another, if successful, only yields an abortion. This is a defect in our graded-school system : each scholar in a class is obliged to pursue the same study as another, and perform the same task, — no more, no less. Can we not remedy the difficulty in the Lyceum ? One child has capabilities for an engineer, one for a poet, one for a painter, one for a geologist, another for a mechanic, and still another for a tradesman; and, recognizing the natural tendencies of each, it should be the aim of the instructor by every persuasive art to develop them. Thus will he touch the mainspring of love and thought, and, true to it, set all the wheels in action.

Do not keep back a scholar who is gifted with clearness of mind, nor unduly crowd those who are mentally sluggish. It were not reasonable to expect the slow-flying jay to cleave the air with the speed of the swallow, nor to chain them together.

What is each best adapted to ? What will render that boy or this girl successful? What will lead out the faculties in the beautiful order which Nature ordained ? — should be leading questions, and primary considerations in all our instructions.

Lend enchantment to the future it is possible for each to attain; awaken practical ideals of duty, and the honor of fidelity to them, whatever may be the chosen sphere of labor. Inspire them with lofty purposes, not poisoned by selfish ambition, but sweetly tempered with the childlike virtues which angels ever cultivate. Give them beautiful views of death, and of the spirit-world, not forgetting its relations to ours, nor the loss attending premature departure from earth. Physical life should be esteemed a blessing, and the health of the body carefully guarded, until the change of worlds shall be natural, and hence desirable.

## *MEMBERSHIP.*

WHEN we assume new social relations, calculated to educate us in our moral responsibilities, and fit us the better for life's great conflicts, as is the beneficent design of the Lyceum, we should enter upon those relations under a most solemn sense of duty and privilege. If undertaken with careless curiosity, as an idle experiment, the interest will droop and die the very first hour of adversity; and, that gone, forms and ceremonials, however beautiful or morally significant as suggestive lessons, will be but irksome tasks, inductive to fault-finding, disunion, and rupture. Aside from this disaster, so mortifying and destructive to our truest affections, such children learn to be irreverent in spirit, and, by habit repeated, soon become vagrant and untrustworthy in character. Nothing is so injurious to the young mind as a careless administration of precept. If we would have our children understand life as it is, and qualify themselves to fulfil its myriad obligations, then impress their tender affections with lofty moral ideals, and lead them by easy methods to their practical utilities. The young love pictures : therefore, let us symbolize the real which we hope to secure after long and patient continuance in well-doing.

Various methods, suggested by existing conditions and circumstances, can be used by ingenious officers to arouse in the minds of members, both young and older, a high moral sense of social responsibility. Productive of the most salutary effect, beautiful introductions might be systematized by the officers and leaders for the reception of members,— as happy addresses, joining of hands in grand circles, singing, Golden-Chain readings and marching, and the presentation of the badges by the guardian of groups, with appropriate remarks. Keeping a book of membership, and calling the roll at the opening of each session, may be used with a happy effect towards inducing punctuality. Let such systems be arranged as the needs of each Lyceum require, of which the proper authorities are the best judges. Let nothing of this kind be stereotyped or made monotonous. The skilful teacher is never at a loss what to do to attract the young mind higher. *Progress!* PROGRESS! is our eternal watchword.

## *CONVERSATIONAL QUESTIONS.*

DISCUSSIONS often exert an unsalutary influence upon the affections: they are apt to be combative, and tainted with the pride of mere opinion. They should never be allowed in the Lyceum. The more natural and conversational our talk with children, the sweeter is the harmony of all concerned. Conversation is better than books. Thought breeds thought, eye speaks to eye, and heart to heart.

In presenting the following questions for Leaders, in as natural and simple a way as possible, we have aimed at orderly and logical argumentation to discipline the young mind. We have outlined these methods merely to awaken ingenuity in others, hoping inspiration may kindle as the occasion needs. Let us have no crystallized forms of education. If what we here do is improved in practice, our object is attained. We submit the questions, and their implied answers, to candid attention.

### LIFE.

Do the trees have life? and the plants and the flowers?
What other things have life?
You say fishes, birds, insects, beasts, human beings, all have life: now, can you mention any thing which has not?
You told me once that spirit and matter, as elemental substances, are indestructible, when in co-action we have a form of life: then, is not life also indestructible? This, then, is my definition: Life is a latent principle in all things; under chemical action of spirit in its material body, this principle is manifest in sentient emotions and consciousness.
As the spirit at death organizes for itself a new body through life-force, life is immortal, — is it not?
How beautiful this is? Please tell me, now, if you can see any analogy between the spirit with its new or heavenly body, and the spirit with its present or earthly body?

PHYSICAL MAN. (*An Illustrative Conversation.*)

*Leader.* — What is man physically?

*William.* — He is an animal; for he has an animal body and instincts.

*Mary.* — I think he is more than an animal, for he loves different from an animal.

*Susan.* — Yes; and he acts different — sometimes.

*William* (laughing). — Much obliged for "*sometimes.*" Susan means a man sometimes gets drunk, and fights and swears: well, that's very animal. Certain horses are more rational and spiritual than some men.

*Susan.* — William likes to drive fine horses, and wants them to be immortal that he may have a like privilege in the spirit-world.

*William.* — Thank you again; and I will invite you, Susan, to take a ride with me through a Summer-Land forest.

*Leader.* — I am sorry to break this thread of happy conversation; but I must say I think you have all forgotten your text: so please come to order, and tell what is man *physical.* Charley is laughing to see that we must come down to *terra firma* again. Well, Charley, I will ask you.

*Charles.* — He is the shell, the garment, the house his spirit inhabits.

*Leader.* — Of what is this house composed? (About this time the bell strikes one, indicating the conversation must close; and the Leader requires William to tell next Sunday what the organs of the body are, Charles to describe the chemical elements of the body, and the girls to inform us how to keep our beautiful house in order. So the lesson has suggested itself for the coming session.)

## RELIGION.

I asked a little girl the other day, what she loved most; and she said, To do good, and make others happy. Now, was not that religion?

Did you ever hear of any form of religion which does not require us to do good?

Then is not the central heart of all religions divine?

The Apostle James says, " Pure and undefiled religion before God and man is this: To visit the widow and fatherless in their affliction, and keep thyself unspotted from the world." How do you like this definition?

Does not religion also recognize a Divine Life?

## HEALTH.

Health is the functional harmony of the spirit and body.

What is disease?

Is the origin of disease spiritual or physical?

What are the natural curatives of disease?

How can disease be prevented?

Does physical disease, in any direction, affect the spiritual body in the after life?

What are the sources of health?

What amusements are conducive to health?
Should we engage in amusements on Sundays?
Are not innocent amusements, on proper occasions, natural methods of worship?
How does the mind affect the health of the body?
Why is the health of the young injured by sleeping with the aged?
What habits and conditions of diet, clothing, habitation, ventilation, and association engender general health?

## DEATH.

Death is the dissolution of copartnership between the physical and spiritual bodies.
Does the process of death impart wisdom?
Is wisdom attainable except through effort and growth?
Is not wisdom indispensable to use and happiness?

## MORAL RATIOS.

Individual identity being as permanent as the law of progress, and moral character being the result of moral action, this life is to the future as childhood to manhood therefore, loss or gain follows wherever we go, and whatever we do.
Are losses and gains eternal?

## ANGELS AND SPIRITS.

Angels and spirits are ascended mortals, who once inhabited this and other planets.
Is there proof of their identical existence prior to their residence on the planets?
In what forms do spirits return to mortals?
What evidence have you that they return?
By what laws and agencies do they make their presence manifest?
To what extent do they retain their love of nationalities?
Where are their habitations?
What is your idea of their location, institutions, and occupations?
Upon what do they subsist?
Do their interests in the earth-life decrease, or increase, in the ratio of their progression?
To what degree are we influenced by ministering spirits?
Is it a voluntary pleasure for them to guard, entrance, and inspire media?
Do they ever peril their moral status by thus descending into our atmosphere?
By what methods can we identify controlling spirits?
Do the highest angels of celestial life control media?
Are there liabilities to mistakes in identification?
What mediumistic conditions are requisite to truthful communications?

## *OBJECT LESSONS.*

OBJECT lessons are doubtless the best method of conveying instruction to the understanding of children; they directly appeal to the senses, which are avenues of knowledge. We therefore respectfully recommend that the ingenious Leader open for delightful inspection the vast arcana of nature and art, and at each session have something new and interesting; always endeavoring to be thorough, leaving the young mind impressed with a recognition of a divine purpose in all things, that the tender affections may be moulded in the likeness of a sweet morality and angelic character. Crystals, pebbles, leaves, grasses, grains, flowers, birds, butterflies, insects, drops of water, colors, odors, fruits of all kinds, fossils, petrifactions, corals, pictures, organs of the human body, — indeed, any thing suggestive of practical thought, are ever appropriate themes of study and discourse in the Lyceum. When the minds of the children are aglow with an earnest enthusiasm, make your moral impressions with all the ardor of your soul.

In order to facilitate the work before us, each Lyceum should be supplied with geographical, geological, astronomical, physiological, and phrenological maps, with pictures of plants and flowers, of animals, insects, fishes, and birds, and of landscape scenery; also with a valuable library and mineral cabinet. Let the walls of our halls be adorned thus with the symbols and relics of natural history. The microscope is an essential instrument; also the spy-glass, the sun-glass, and the telescope.

We subjoin a few object-lessons, not as finalities, but simply as illustrations. Let the Leader procure a living or preserved butterfly, and proceed at once to instruct, with varied ingenuity, just as the occasion may suggest, of which the following may be a natural outline: —

### THE BUTTERFLY.

What is this?
What are its beautiful colors?
How many eyes has it?
Why does it need so many eyes?
See! does it have any feet?
Does it fly, or walk?
How many wings has it?
If the butterfly has wings and can fly, can it not do more than you can?
Then would you not like to be a butterfly?
Did it always fly like a bird?
What was it before it was a butterfly?
Did it fly then?
What kind of a motion did it make?
What did it live on?
Was it as pretty then as it is now?

# LESSONS FROM FAMILIAR OBJECTS.

Did you ever tread on a caterpillar?
Would you have killed it had you then known it would ever be a butterfly?
What made it a butterfly?
What is a cocoon?
How did it make its cocoon?
How long did it stay in its little house?
How did it liberate itself?
Did you ever see a chrysalis?
What makes its shell so tough?
When a chrysalis, was the little creature dead?
Does your body bear any relation to a caterpillar?
The chrysalis concealed the butterfly in embryo: now, what does your body likewise conceal?
What did you say the caterpillar lived upon?
What do you live upon?
After the butterfly is developed, and escapes from its chrysalis, what does it live upon?
After you leave your body, what will you?
If you injure a caterpillar or its chrysalis, will not the future butterfly be feeble? Will it be healthful and beautiful?
If you injure your body by intemperance or neglect, will it not depress or darken your spirit?
What should we do to be happy here and hereafter?

## THE PEBBLE.

Can you tell me what this is? Take it in your hand and examine it?
A piece of rock, is it? But what kind of rock?
To what geological period does it belong?
Look at its shade: what made it so?
See its color: what is it?
Did it grow?
How old is it, think you?
Now, there is a strange history about this pebble, written all over it: can you read it?
Well, I knew you could not see any letters on it; but each of you hold it a moment calmly and patiently in your hand, and then tell me what your sensations and impressions are.
Here the Leader can discourse with success upon the laws of psychometry, and thus with varied and frequent experiments happily develop this beautiful gift in the minds of the group, and show them how to be *themselves* the history of the universe.

# PHYSICAL PERFECTION.

THOSE glorious old pagans, the Greeks, from whom, in spite of our boasted modern civilization, we have still so much to learn, appreciated more fully than any other nation since their time the importance of physical culture; which they made the foundation of their whole system of education. They evidently were not "ashamed of their bodies;" but rather glorified in them as tenements worthy of the indwelling soul. All the young men of the nation were trained in manly exercises. The simple crown of green leaves which was placed upon the brow of the victor in their noble athletic games, under the eyes of his assembled countrymen and countrywomen, was more coveted by the Grecian youth than the diadem of the king. It was not only a crown of glory for himself, but gave renown to the city in which he was born.

It was in the gymnasium, and at the Pythian, Nemean, and Olympic games, that the sure foundations of an integral development were deeply and strongly laid in the most complete and systematic bodily culture. Philosophy, oratory, poetry, music, painting, and sculpture, formed a fitting superstructure. It was also in the gymnasium and at the national games that Plato, Aristotle, and the other philosophers, lectured and taught, conversing with their pupils as they rested from their exercises, carrying along mental with physical training.

And now, to bring it to the true test, where was the result of the Greek educational system? Undoubtedly the finest race the world ever saw grew up under it, — the strongest and bravest men, and the most beautiful women (for the physical culture of the latter was not neglected), — philosophers, poets, orators, and sculptors which the modern world has never equalled.

## *CALISTHENICS.*

THIS term is derived from two Greek words, signifying beauty and strength, and embraces those gymnastic exercises more especially adapted to the public hall, or school. Their introduction into the Lyceum has several objects in view. They throw off the physical restlessness of the children, while furnishing them with amusement; they teach the grand lesson that physical and mental culture should go hand in hand;

# CALISTHENICS. 157

they harmonize the minds of the participants, and provide the means of thorough education of the muscles in graceful movement to the mandates of the will. Half of education is to give the mind this perfect gracefulness; ease of action depends upon it: awkwardness results from its defects. In no manner is it possible to attain this result so perfectly as by calisthenic movements simultaneously executed to music. Although the exercise is practised but once a week, it tones the muscular system for the entire intermediate period; and those who comprehend its purpose can practise at any time. The Conductor should impress the members with the necessity of promptness, decision, and grace in all the movements. If executed in an awkward, thoughtless manner, their influence is not only lost, but pernicious.

The exercises here introduced have been selected and arranged from various sources with the view to give only such as the most fastidious could not object to. They have been tested in the Lyceum by long experience, and found desirable. Practically, any movement which is in itself ungraceful and distorting cannot be introduced. Shrugging the shoulders, kicking, or twisted positions of head or body, will not be received by the higher groups, and in the public hall are offensive to refined taste.

As the first lesson in these Exercises, the Conductor should teach the correct manner of sitting and standing. Three strokes of the bell call all to their feet. The members should stand far enough apart not to interfere with each other, and in straight lines, not only across the hall, but in the opposite direction.

1st *Command.* — ATTENTION: The position is that of a soldier. The feet near together; the toes turning slightly outward; body and head erect; and the arms by the sides.

2d *Command.* — FOLD ARMS.
3d *Command.* — REVERSE ARMS.
4th *Command.* — REST ARMS. (See Figure No. 5.)
5th *Command.* — ARMS FREE. (By the side.)

We have divided the exercises into four series; each of which is preceded by the *Wand Movement.* They can be used in their order for the four Sundays of the month, or two or more at the same session, as the Conductor may judge best. While promptness and perfection is desirable, the object of the Lyceum is not wholly to learn Calisthenics and Marching. They are only means to certain ends, and should not occupy more than fifteen minutes each, at the extreme.

## WAND MOVEMENTS.

6th *Command.* — POSITION FOR WAND MOVEMENTS: Position erect, with the right hand resting in the left, as seen in Fig. 1, at $d$.

The music now plays the first strain of some tune written in double or quadruple time. This it repeats; and, at the first beat of the repeat, the right arm is extended to $a$; at the second, to $b$; at the third, to $c$; at the fourth, returned to position at $d$. This is repeated. The left hand is then carried through the arcs $a'$, $b$, $c'$, and returned. Then both hands execute these movements simultaneously, and repeat.

The hands should move in curves, as represented in the Figure. At *a a'* the palms should be horizontal; at *c c'*, their inner edge should be presented in front; at *b*, the

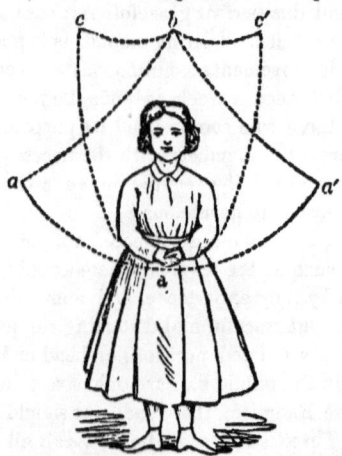

FIG. 1.—POSITION FOR WAND MOVEMENTS.

palms should be in front, the fore-fingers and thumbs brought nearly in contact. The body should participate in the movement of the arms.

## FIRST SERIES.

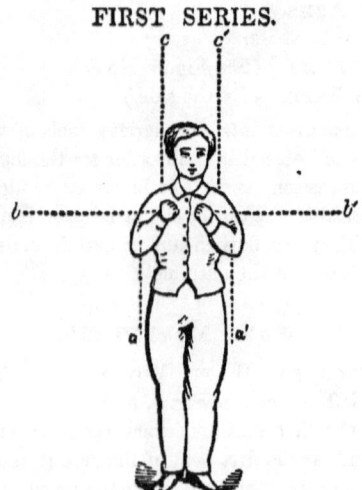

FIG. 2.—POSITION FOR CALISTHENICS.

7th *Command*.— POSITION FOR CALISTHENICS: Position of a soldier, except the hands are clenched on the breast.

## PHYSICAL PERFECTION. 159

1. Music plays the first strain, and repeats. At the first beat, the right hand is thrust downward to *a* (Fig. 2); at the second, returned; at the third, down; at the fourth, returned. This movement should be executed by bending the arm only at the elbow.

At the next beat, thrust the left hand down to *a'*; at the second, return. Repeat.

At the next beat, thrust the right hand down to *a*; at the next, bring it to position, and thrust the left down to *a'* simultaneously; at the next, reverse by thrusting the left to position, and thrusting the right down; at the fourth, bring the right to position. *This is the alternate movement.* At the next beat, thrust both downward simultaneously to *a a'*; return; repeat.

2. Extend the right arm horizontally to *b*; return. Repeat. Left arm the same to *b'*; return. Repeat. Alternate twice; simultaneously twice.

FIG. 3.    FIG. 4.

3. Extend right arm directly upward to *c*; return; repeat. Left arm the same to *c'*. Alternate twice; simultaneously twice.

4. Extend right arm directly in front; return. Repeat. Left the same. Alternate twice; simultaneously twice.

5. Thrust the right arm down to *a* (Fig. 2); return; thrust it upward to *c*; return. Repeat. Thrust the left downward to *a'*; return. Thrust it upward to *c'*; return. Repeat. Altenate twice; both down simultaneously; return. Both up; return.

6. Thrust the right arm to the left (Fig. 3), *a*; return; thrust to right as seen in Fig. 4, *b*; return. Repeat. Left arm the same.

7. Turn to the right, thrusting both arms to right, keeping the feet firmly in place, and twisting the body; return. Turn to the left, thrusting the arms in that direction. Turn to the right, thrusting the arms as before, twice; to the left, twice.

8. Return to position. Thrust both down; return. Both out; return. Both up; return. Both front; return to position of *Attention*; bow twice.

## SECOND SERIES.

*Position.* — REST ARMS, as in Figure 5.

FIG. 5.

1. Step to the right with the right foot, — from *a* to *b*, in Fig. 6, — follow with the left; return with left; follow with the right. Repeat four times.

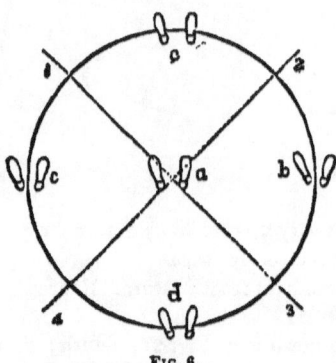

FIG. 6.

2. Step to left with the left foot, — from *a* to *c*; follow with the right; return with right, and follow with the left. Repeat four times.
3. Step backward with the right foot, — from *a* to *d*; follow with left. Return with right foot, and follow with the left. Repeat four times.
4. Step forward with the right foot, — from *a* to *c*; follow with the left. Return with right foot, and follow with the left. Repeat four times, at the last beat returning to position shown in Figure 7, bringing the points of the fingers in a line with, and pointing towards, the shoulders. The shoulders should be thrown well back.

## PHYSICAL PERFECTION. 161

5. Extend the right arm to *a;* return; repeat four times. Left, the same to *a'*. Alternate four times; simultaneously four times. At the last beat, bring the palms of the hands together, directly in front, the arms being extended forward horizontally, as

FIG. 7.

in Figure 8, *a*. Then, keeping the arms rigid, except at the shoulders, swing them through the circle, — the first beat from *a* to *b;* the second, from *b* to *a;* repeating.

FIG. 8.

6. Reverse the motion, passing from *a* to *b* in the opposite direction; repeating four times. At the last beat, bringing the hands to breast, as in Figure 4.
7. At the next beat, extend both down, simultaneously, — repeat; out, — repeat; up, — repeat; front, — repeat.
8. Slap the hands four times, and bow twice.

11

## THIRD SERIES.

*Position.* — REST ARMS. Figure No. 5.

1. At the first beat, step with the right foot back (Fig. 6. from *a* to *d*), follow with the left; return with right, and follow with left. Repeat.
2. Step forward with right foot (from *a* to *c*), follow with the left; return with right, follow with left. Repeat.
3. Oblique step, backward to right, with right foot (Fig. 6, from *a* to 3), follow with left; return with right, and follow with left.
4. Oblique, backward to left (from *a* to 4).
5. Oblique, forward to right (from *a* to 2).
6. Oblique, forward to left (from *a* to 1). Movements 4, 5, 6, are performed similarly to No. 3.
7. Beat twice with the right heel; charge to the left: return. Repeat. The position of charge is shown in figure 9.

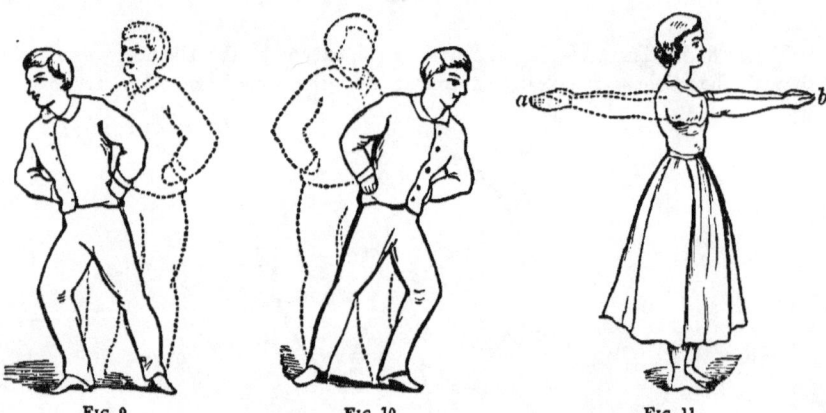

FIG. 9.   FIG. 10.   FIG. 11.

8. Beat twice with the left heel, charge to the right; return. Repeat. The two positions are perfectly explained in the above diagrams. At last beat bring hands to the breast (Fig. 2).
9. Thrust the right arm downward; at the second beat, open the hand; at the third, clench the hand; at the fourth, return to position. Repeat. The same with the left arm. Simultaneously. The same movement, outward, upward, and forward. At the last beat, bring the palms of the hands in contact, the arms thrust horizontally forward as in Figure 11, *b*.
10. Keep the arms rigid except at the shoulders, and at the next beat carry them directly backward, so that their backs may touch as near as possible, as at *a*, in Fig. 11. Return at the next beat. Repeat four times, on the last beat returning to position for the wand movement, and completing the measure by slapping the hands.

# PHYSICAL PERFECTION.

## FOURTH SERIES.

*Position.* — ATTENTION.

1. At the first beat, throw the hands upward, as in Figure 12. At the second, return. Repeat four times. At the last beat, clasp the hands behind the back.
2. Thrust them downward; return. Repeat four times. At the last beat, clasp the hands on the breast.
3. Carry them down as far as possible without unclasping; return. Repeat four times. At the last beat, bring the hands to position of Rest Arms (Fig. 5).
4. Stamp the right foot, then the left; step out with right foot in position of charge (Figs. 9 and 10); return. Repeat four times.
5. The same with the left foot.

FIG. 12.    FIG. 13.

6. Draw the right elbow back as far as possible, throwing the chest forward and inhaling. Repeat. Left the same. Alternately twice. Simultaneously twice. At the last beat, bring the hands to the breast as in Figure 2.
7. Thrust the right arm down, with the back of the hand in front; twist the hand outward; back; return to first position. Repeat. Left hand the same. Alternately twice. Simultaneously twice. Same movements outward, upward, and front. At the last beat, extend the arms in position represented in Figure 13.
8. At the next beat, bend to the right, as represented in Figure 14, *c d;* at the next, to the left, as in *a b*. Repeat four times, bringing the hands into position of Rest Arms at the last beat (Fig. 5).

9. Turn the body to the right, partially bowing in doing so; return. Repeat. Turns to the left. Repeat. Alternate once, bringing hands to the side at the last beat.

FIG. 14.

10. Bow to complete the measure.

NOTE. — Singing while executing the wand movement, Calisthenic exercises, or while marching, produces a very pleasing effect. There are several songs in the collection suitable for this purpose; but "Sing All Together," on page 47, has been prepared expressly for wand movements, or Calisthenics.

## MARCHING.

THE object of marching is not only to afford amusement, but to inculcate promptness of action, and grace of movement. Like Calisthenics, it should not be made an end, but a means; and the officers of the Lyceum should be very careful that neither are introduced in excess. Fifteen minutes should be the extreme time consumed in marching. When these exercises are given more time, it must be done at the expense of the intellectual, the most important, and the real object of the Lyceum sessions. The temptation is very strong, as at first they are amusing; but very soon weariness is produced, and apathy takes the place of interest. The marching admits of almost endless diversity; and the conductor can vary it to the necessities of his Lyceum, or the capabilities of his hall. The methods here introduced are only suggestive. The main points are to teach accurate time in keeping step, and precision in direct marching; and the appropriate manner of carrying the banners, so that in processions, and all public occasions, proper order and beauty may be preserved.

The banners should be placed to the right of the conductor's stand; the banners of the leaders to the left. The guards hand them out as the members pass. The banner should always be received with the left hand, then grasp the end of the staff with the right, which bring straight to the side, the staff touching the shoulder. This should be strictly enforced, as nothing gives the marching a worse appearance than having the flags carried in a disorderly manner.

Fig. 15, on page 172, shows the proper position. It will be seen that it is held in the same manner as a pen.

The standard-bearers may execute a march first, and, depositing their standards, receive banners with the others; or they may march around the hall once, and then the members of the Lyceum follow them. In the latter case, the conductor gives this order: STANDARD-BEARERS, TO POSITION. They, having been already selected by the leaders from their respective groups, advance to the right aisle, from their position in the centre of their groups, and stand facing the conductor in a line; at the command, MARCH, the guardian who is by the side of the standard-bearer of the highest group advances, and is followed by the standard-bearers in double column; when they have passed nearly around the hall, three strokes of the bell calls all to their feet, and the groups join the procession as it passes, in double column. When it approaches the conductor, one of the guards hands the leaders their banners; and, as it passes, other guards hand the members theirs. A great variety of movements will suggest themselves; and, if the Lyceum is fortunate in the possession of a large hall, these may be varied to almost any extent.

## The Arcade of Standards

is thus formed: when the standard-bearers pass the conductor's stand, he commands, HALT. STANDARD-BEARERS, ATTENTION. FORM — ARCADE. At this command, the right column steps one step to the right, the left one step to the left, elevate their standards, and bring them in contact overhead. The command is now given, DEPRESS BANNERS — MARCH! and the procession passes through the arcade. The space between the guardian and the procession must be preserved; and, when she again passes through, it will just approach the entrance. Then the command is given, STANDARD-BEARERS, MARCH; and they fall into rank.

Another beautiful movement is thus executed: the command is, HALT. RIGHT COLUMN ONE STEP TO RIGHT, — LEFT TO LEFT. GUARDIAN, ABOUT FACE. RIGHT AND LEFT, COUNTER-MARCH. It is fully explained by the command.

## THE GOLDEN CHAIN.

To execute this, the procession is formed in single file, and one of the guards numbers the members thus, as they pass: the first is one, the next two, the next one, the next two, and so to the last. The command is given: FIRST RANK, — ONE STEP TO RIGHT. At this order, all those whose number is one step to right. At the next command, FIRST RANK, — COUNTER — MARCH, — the column thus formed moves forward, while the second remains stationary, following the guardian, who passes to the left of the first, the right of the second, the left of the third, and in this manner to the last, when she counter-marches to the left, bringing the column into its first position, and halts. The next command is, SECOND RANK, COUNTER-MARCH; when the guardian leads them through the same winding course between the members of the first, bringing them to position in the same manner. This march is emblematical of the fraternal regards and blending of feeling between the members, and is extremely beautiful. When the platform will admit, counter-marching executed thereon is also very beautiful. The seats in the hall must be movable, and the guards set them aside. Counter-marching, or marching in single, double, or quadruple file, can then be easily executed.

When the time assigned for marching has expired, the guards receive the banners as the procession passes, and it counter-marches in front of the conductor's stand. He then orders, FRONT FACE; and a song or golden chain being executed, five strokes of the bell, twice repeated, dismisses the Lyceum. This pre-supposes that the marching is the last exercise; which, for reason of the removing of the seats, it is most convenient to make it. If it is not, and the seats have not been removed, the procession may march to their respective places.

When the seats are arranged with a central and side aisles, a fine effect may be produced by the conductor *and* guardian, or assistants, leading the procession in double column up the central aisle, dividing, and each separate column passing down the side aisles, meeting again at the point from whence they started, or by dividing right and left by twos; at that point they unite in fours, and march in that manner up the central aisle.

There should be as few commands as possible; and, after the Lyceum is thoroughly drilled, the commands will not be sufficiently noticeable to give a disagreeable military impression to the exercise.

The conductor should insist on promptness, precision, and order. The time should be marked by the step, at least one strain, before the command, MARCH, is given. A triangle accompaniment is very useful, or the spring-bell will answer every purpose in marking time.

### THE BELL.

A spring-bell is indispensable in the Lyceum. It not only calls to order; its silver tone is the easiest method of preserving it, and its signals the most readily given and understood. The following signals will be found serviceable:—

Five strokes of the bell calls all to order.
Four " " " " " to be seated.
Three " " " " " to their feet.
Two " " " " " officers to their feet.
One " " " is the signal for order.
Five " repeated, dismisses the Lyceum.

## PROGRAMME FOR A LYCEUM SESSION.

### PART FIRST.

1. At the bell-signal, the groups assemble, and all officers at once take their respective places.
2. The guardian and her assistant distribute the Group Books, Badges, and the books used by the school.
3. New names entered, badges put on, books in hand.
4. Singing by the whole Lyceum.

### PART SECOND.

1. Golden Chain Recitations.
2. Calisthenics.
3. Conversation on the lesson, throughout the groups.
4. Reports from the groups on the question before the assembly.
5. Proposal and adoption of questions or subjects for new lessons.

### PART THIRD.

1. Declamations; brief readings; music, vocal or instrumental, by individual members.
2. A lecture or lesson on some educational topic, by the conductor, guardian, or some chosen person.
3. The removal of the badges.

### PART FOURTH.

1. Leaders select standard-bearers for the grand march, who quietly take positions in the aisle at the head of the groups they respectively represent, in line.
2. The guardian, with her banner, having taken her place opposite the standard-bearer of the highest group, marches, at the signal of the conductor, down the aisle, the standard-bearers falling in as she passes them, one after another.
3. At the bell-signal, all arise; and, as the guardian and standard-bearers pass, join successively in the march, commencing with the highest group. The guards give out the banners while the school is marching, and they are returned to the same while marching in rank, just before counter-marching in front of the conductor's stand.
4. Singing or Recitation.
5. Adjournment.

### REMARKS ON THE PROGRAMME.

*Part First.* Be prompt but quiet in obeying the signals. Be respectful to your leaders, and willing to do as they recommend you in taking part in the exercises. Take your places every session, resolved to learn all you can, and *do* all you can to interest and instruct others. Do not neglect your duty as a Lyceum member, of *taking part in all the exercises*, because you may have a mood of disinclination. There should be unity of soul and action.

The Badges should be worn on the left breast.

The singing should be general. If you *cannot* sing, be one in soul with those who are singing; find the song in your book, look over, try to learn.

*Part Second.* The Golden Chain Recitation is executed by the alternate reading of the conductor, the groups, and other officers; the conductor leading, and the rest responding, led by the guardian. Care and practice should be given to effect the utterance of the responses in unison.

The leaders should stand at the head of their classes during Calisthenics, forming a straight line down the hall.

The leader should converse affectionately and with simplicity on the topic with the group under his charge, drawing out their opinions encouragingly, and, if the general question is beyond their understanding, select one more simple. It is desirable that each member give a brief answer to the question: the member should arise in his seat, and report to the conductor in a distinct, courteous manner, so that all in the hall may hear. The responses are often more interesting than the most learned lecture. It is a very good way to secure carefully-selected subjects for lessons, to have one person chosen every Sunday to bring in two or three questions for consideration, which are presented to the Lyceum, and the one desired chosen by vote. Then there is no danger of having trifling and unprofitable questions accepted in consequence of haste and carelessness.

*Part Third.* In many places, particularly country places where the societies are small, it is impossible to provide a good lecturer every Sunday; the expense is too great, and cannot be borne. By effort and study, the Lyceum may afford a rich intellectual feast at each session, and prove a means of growth as well as pleasure. Learn to render your readings and declamations artistically. You can get books which will teach you these things at home, if you have patience to study them. The rules and training contained in "Voice and Action," by J. E. Frobisher, are excellent, and will make you healthy as well as graceful orators. A beautiful song or a piece of instrumental music is always acceptable. How many times the strains of music are reproduced in our minds during the week, always softening and sanctifying us. Much and careful attention should be given to the internal growth of societies: it is this which will make them healthful and permanent.

Punctuality should be inculcated. The conductor should call the Lyceum to order at precisely the appointed time. There should be promptness and decision in all the exercises, and no delays by which the sessions are made tedious.

## *PROMOTIONS.*

NATURE is progressive. All things unfold upward in orderly use, from root to flower, from flower to fruit. Planets and suns are as lilies, blossoming on the ocean of infinitude. In several degrees, the whole universe presses close to the divine, — the heart of the Spirit beating the cycles of progress forever. Feeling the springs of life ever flowing to us, ever widening from us, we instinctively love improvement. As the human body is a "house of many mansions," so the mind is keyed to many plans of thought, and naturally ascends from rudimental principles to transfigurations, "from glory to glory." When we have made one circuit of investigation, turn not back again, for that *now* is an old track; but commence another, laden with the trophies of the first. Incorporating with the new whatever truth the past has revealed, press we on is our right, heeding the angel's call, — "Come up higher!" Let a child understand there is yet a brighter light ahead, a more beautiful truth to learn, a higher life to live, — enforce this fact by a happy example, — and the Lyceum becomes a very charm, exhaustless in interest, like Nature prolific with beauty, advancing into loftier circles of love to coronate the whole being in divinity of character. The ingenious instructor is ever devising methods by which to call out the slumbering energies of childhood. No set rules will answer this purpose for all time. Pecuniary rewards, as incentives to action, may be a questionable morality; for they foster jealousy and self-interest. Cannot the virtues of life be presented in so beautiful an aspect as to be of themselves rewards for well-doing? Show the child that fidelity to principle is the pathway to heaven, and heaven will never be sought through the carnal motives of fear or selfish hope. If we would educate children to be angels, awaken angels' love in their affections, — love of truth for its own intrinsic worth.

Let us endeavor, therefore, to demonstrate to our children that every new truth learned, every virtue gained, every moral victory over self and temptation, is a promotion, is a progress, the best rewards of which are a happier and better life, and higher qualification for the society of angels.

## *CELEBRATIONS.*

IT was the custom of the ancients to celebrate the changes of the seasons with religious festivities. What is more appropriate for us? From Nature we get all our true lessons. Why not commemorate the changes of her progressive revolutions? Infancy is our Spring of budding hopes; youth is our Summer of unfolding into love and beauty; Autumn is the manhood and womanhood of life, the harvest of virtue, the ripening for the Spirit-World; Winter is snowy age, when the patient, waiting soul should be morally white as the vestures of angels; it is the day when the gates of mortality close behind the spirit, and the portals of heaven noiselessly unfold. It is well to celebrate these days. While the "holy days" of the Church are artificial, ever looking back to the dead past, let ours be natural festivities, blessing the living present.

Let our spring festival be the 31st of March, commemorative of the Spirit Rappings, which, in Rochester, N.Y., 1848, inaugurated the Spiritual Dispensation. The Executive Board may arrange for lectures, music, embracing choruses of rejoicing, devise dramatic scenes illustrative of the event, and will be at no loss to frame a programme of inspiring exercises.

The summer solstice is on the 21st of June: it is the longest day in the year, and therefore has most light. Summer has then fully come, and the spring flowers are in bloom. A more appropriate day cannot be chosen for a floral celebration. Then it is expected the hall will be beautifully adorned with flowers, and the exercises of the most exhilarating order, such as marching, singing, dancing, crowning the Standards with floral wreaths, and presenting bouquets to the officers with appropriate addresses. The conveniences and circumstances of the occasion must, of course, determine the exercises.

On the 22d of September, the length of the days and nights is equal. It is the day of balance in nature, the inauguration of the harvest. We call it the Astronomical Celebration. The last flowers of Summer, and the first fruits of Autumn, should be brought, for adornments, to the hall; the last blooms of Summer, the golden sheaf of wheat, the early apple, and the ripened plum, the beautiful, blushing peaches, the luscious grape, should be arranged in the centre of the hall; the children may circle around the table of treasures, holding hands and dancing, singing in merry voices. Other amusements and instructive lessons should be devised to render this day one of the happiest of the year. The innocent mind may be thus impressed by showing that the soul blossoms and ripens for the harvest which is to come.

On the 25th of January, 1863, in Dodworth's Hall, New-York City, Andrew Jackson Davis delivered his first address on the Lyceum system. What the angels had revealed to him was there formed into practical order. There it was that he organized the first Children's Progressive Lyceum ever known in the history of our world. The event is replete with golden memories. We should keep it fresh in our affections by an annual festival, to be called the Lyceum Celebration.

## *LYCEUM ANNIVERSARY.*

THE anniversary of the Lyceum is an auspicious occasion. To close the old, and enter upon the new, invigorates every latent force, and inspires fresh ambition for improvement. It should, therefore, be commemorated with exercises that recall the trials and victories of the past, and that kindle loftier purposes for the future.

Few are qualified for office: those who are should serve. The lovers of children, apt in instruction, punctual and orderly in habit, happy in address, pure in example are Nature's nobility, and the servants for rulership. Personal ambition for position, a disposition to rule or ruin, blasts like the mildew every sunny hope of success in a Lyceum. How charming are the qualities of humility, high-toned morality, intellectual purity, and simplicity of manner!

We recommend a term of three months only for the officers; and, if they proved worthy, they can be re-elected. The children, mainly, are the electors. They should always be consulted, especially in the choice of their Leaders, which office is, *in fact*, the highest of the Lyceum.

Aside from the usual amusements and sociabilities of such occasions, appropriate addresses and songs are expected. An impressive form of installation, such as the officers might arrange, would add new interest to the work. This would give scope to ingenuity, and the freshness of inspiration at every step of responsibility. Order and system are what we need, with studious care to avoid taxing ceremonials, and the monotony of constant repetition.

## *BANNER EXERCISES.*

THE Lyceum should be drawn up in two lines facing each other; counter-marched in parallel columns and ranks in front of the conductor, or, if on exhibition, on the platform. It must be remembered, that in these exercises, as well as in marching,

FIG. 15.

the first word of the command is preparatory; and sufficient pause should be made before the final word, which is the real command; and no movement should be made until this last is given, unless otherwise directed.

The preceding cut shows the first position.

1. *Shoulder — Banners.* — The feet are brought near together, the toes turning slightly outward; the body erect; shoulders thrown back; the arms extended by the sides; the right hand holding the end of the staff between the thumb and forefinger after the manner of a pen; bringing it firmly against the shoulder in a perfectly erect position.

2. *Present — Banners.* — Grasp the centre of the staff with the left hand; at the command, move the right, so as to bring the staff directly in front, preserving it in perpendicular manner.

3. *Shoulder — Banners.* — Carry it back to its first position, then drop the left arm to the side.

4. *Support — Banners.* — Bring the right hand just below the left breast, preserving the perpendicularity of the staff; bring the left fore-arm across the staff at nearly right angle; at the last word, drop the right hand to place.

5. *Shoulder — Banners.* — Grasp the end of the staff with the right hand; drop the left to place, and bring the banner to position.

6. *Order — Banners.* — Grasp the staff in the centre with the left hand, at the preparatory word; bring the right hand to the top, and, at the command, bring the end of the staff to the floor, slightly in front, keeping it erect.

7. *Parade — Rest.* — Step back with the right foot, bringing it to a slight angle with the left, and lay the left hand on top of the right.

8. *Attention.* — Resume position of *Order Banners.*

9. *Shoulder — Banners.* — Grasp the staff or the centre with the left hand; drop the right to place; bring the banner to position; grasp it with the right, and drop the left to place.

10. *Carry — Banners.* — Raise the right hand to hip, preserving the staff erect.

11. *Shoulder — Banners.* — Drop the right arm to place.

12. *Parry — Banners.* — Raise the staff in a horizontal position a little higher than the eye, with the right hand, which holds it by the end. The flag-end of the staff must be thrown slightly forward to avoid interference with the one on the left.

13. *Shoulder — Banners.* — Carry Banners in a circle over the head, bringing to position.

14. *Trail — Banners.* — Grasp the staff with the left hand, near the flag; bring the right hand up to it; drop the left hand to place, and carry the right down to its position.

15. *Shoulder — Banners.* — Bring the right hand up to the hip; grasp the staff above it; slide the right hand down to the end of staff. At the word Banner, drop left arm to place, and bring staff to position.

16. *Depress — Banners.* — Let the staff slide downward through the hand until its top is just above the shoulder.

17. *Shoulder — Banners.* — Grasp staff with left hand, raise it to place, and return to position.

18. *Port — Banners.* — This can only be executed when marching in double columns. The staffs are crossed in the centre, just below the banners.

19. *Shoulder — Banners.* — Bring banners to position. These exercises may be executed by the standard-bearers, and form an interesting diversion.

*W. H. Saxton.*

## FUNERAL SERVICES.

TO those who believe in the religion of Spiritualism, death is perhaps less terrible than to those of any other faith. To them he comes, not as an enemy, draped in folds of midnight blackness, but as a friend, whose face is beaming with hope and cheering promises. To the material senses he is, however, always a mournful friend. They greet him with trembling lips and tearful eyes. They cannot look beyond the physical wreck to the triumphant existence of the liberated angel. A veil has dropped between them and an object of their love, behind which all is silence and mystery.

They must have their expressions of grief, — their moanings, their doubtings, their tears. These are natural; and we cannot hope, with any expectation, to rise entirely above their dominion. But let us bring to these funeral days all the balm and beauty which our religion affords. Let life and immortality be sounded in triumphant and solemn music. Bring cheerful flowers to do their mission of relief and prophecy. Let us say the "Good-night," sadly if we must, but hopefully, facing the sunlight of heaven, and reading promises of continued life, individuality, friendship, communion.

A few suggestions may be offered concerning the method of conducting funerals, which are based on the principles of Spiritualism and the reality of life beyond the grave.

If the departed be a member of the Lyceum, or if it be requested that the mortal part be buried with Lyceum ceremonials, let the emblems and external tokens be first arranged.

The many Lyceums throughout our land have originated some very beautiful and tender ceremonies. From these, and our own tastes, we will offer a few suggestions.

The standard of the group from which the member has ascended may be draped with white crape, fastened with evergreen, and white flowers.

The members of the group, and the leader, may wear a knot of white fastened on the left breast by a sprig of evergreen; or, if it be thought best, the entire Lyceum may do so as well as the group. During the service, two of the guards should sit, one at the head and one at the foot of the coffin, facing the assembly. They should not take part in the reading or singing of the occasion, but be silent and watchful, tenderly guarding the unoccupied coffin. The exercises may commence with appropriate singing, which may be followed by Golden-chain recitations.

A not too lengthy lecture, touching on things which breathe to the mourning hope and consolation, and remind us of the beautiful beatitudes which death bestows upon its subject, is desirable. We are too apt to forget them in our selfish sorrow, and it is well that they be repeated to us when we most deeply need their balm.

Then may come the last look upon the dead face, each group passing out in order, followed by its leader, passing on slowly and quietly around the hall, until all take their seats again.

When all is ready, and the music, playing a solemn and impressive march, leads the procession to the burial-place, the Lyceum should march with depressed banners, but not with depressed standards. When the grave is reached and the coffin lowered, while the members form a circle around it, let each group and leader advance and cast into the tomb a sprig of evergreen, as an emblem of undying friendship. Then, restoring the circle, the conductor and guardian standing at the head of the grave, the conductor may say, —

Dust to dust.

*Members.* — Even so. Dust to dust.

*Con.* — Where is our missing member?

*Mem.* — Not here in the grave, but arisen.

*Con.* — He dwells in the Better Land;

*Mem.* — Whither we all are going.

*Con.* — Then let us say " Good-night," —

*Mem.* — Tearfully, lovingly, hopefully!

*Con.* — Good-night, brother. [Or sister.]

*Mem.* — Good-night, brother.

*All.* — We shall meet again in the morning, where the day endureth forever and forever.

## SONG OF THE SILENT LAND.

#### 1.

INTO the Silent Land!
Ah! who shall lead us thither?
Clouds in the evening sky more darkly gather,
And shattered wrecks lie thicker on the strand.
Who leads us with a gentle hand
Thither, oh! thither,
Into the Silent Land?

#### 2.

Into the Silent Land!
To you, ye boundless regions
Of all perfection! Tender morning visions
Of beauteous souls! The Future's pledge and bond,
Who in life's battle firm doth stand
Shall bear Hope's tender blossoms
Into the Silent Land.

## 3.

O Land! O Land!
For all the broken-hearted,
The mildest herald of our fate allotted
Beckons, and with inverted torch doth stand
To lead us with a gentle hand
Into the land of the great Departed,
Into the Silent Land.

## FAREWELLS.

*All.* — Farewell to thee, blighted bud!
*Con.* — The peace and purity and stillness of death have fallen upon thy unfolding beauties.
*Mem.* — But the sweetness and love and glory of heaven have dawned upon the spirit which dwelt in thee.
*Con.* This form, which knew only a brief existence, reposes in the arms of night, dark and fathomless.
*Mem.* — The spirit, which is indestructible and deathless, lives in the light of heaven, growing more blessed and resplendent forever and forever.
*Con.* — O Death! forever old, forever irresistible.
*Mem.* — One by one generations follow thee away into the land where sweet lips never turn to dust, nor dear eyes to ashes.
*Con.* — O beautiful, beautiful land!
*Mem.* — O angel dwellers in light!
*Con.* — To thy care we commend the spirit we could no longer keep.
*Mem.* — Bless it with the treasure of thy stainless love!
*All.* — And while we turn tearfully from this parting, it is to dream confidently of the new and bright existence of one we love. Farewell!

## RESIGNATION.

### 1.

THE air is full of farewells to the dying,
    And mournings for the dead:
The heart of Rachel, for her children crying,
    Will not be comforted.

### 2.

Let us be patient! These severe afflictions
    Not from the ground arise,
But oftentimes celestial benedictions
    Assume this dark disguise.

**3.**

We see but dimly through the mists and vapors:
　Amid these earthly damps,
What seem to us but sad, funereal tapers
　May be heaven's distant lamps.

**4.**

There is no death! What seems so is transition.
　This life of mortal breath
Is but a suburb of the life elysian,
　Whose portal we call Death.

**5.**

In that great cloister's stillness and seclusion,
　By guardian angels led,
Safe from temptation, safe from sin's pollution,
　They live whom we call dead.

**6.**

We will be patient, and assuage the feeling
　We may not wholly stay:
By silence sanctifying, not concealing,
　The grief that must have way.

## LIFE WILL ATTAIN ITS COMPLETENESS.

*Con.* — O child! O new-born denizen of life's great city!
*Mem.* — On thy head the glory of the morn is shed, like a celestial benison!
*Con.* — Here at the portal thou dost stand, and with thy little hand,
*Mem.* — Thou openest the mysterious gate
　　Into the future's undiscovered land.
*Con.* — Like the new moon thy life appears,
*Mem.* — A little strip of silver light.
*Con.* — And yet, upon its outer rim,
　　A luminous circle, faint and dim,
　　And scarcely visible to us here,
　　Rounds and completes the perfect sphere.
*Mem* — A prophecy and intimation,
　　A pale and feeble adumbration,
　　Of the great world of life that lies
　　Beyond all human destinies.

## YIELDING UP THE FORM.

**1.**

TAKE it, O Death! and bear away
  Whatever thou canst call thine own:
Thine image stamped upon the clay,
  Doth give thee that, but that alone.

**2.**

Take it, O Grave! and let it lie
  Folded upon thy narrow shelves,
A garment by the soul lain by,
  And precious only to ourselves.

**3.**

Take it, O great Eternity!
  Our little life is but a gust
That bends the branches of thy tree,
  And trails its blossoms in the dust.

## THE NIGHT IS BRIEF.

I PLEDGE you in this cup of grief,
  Where floats the fennel's bitter leaf,
The Battle of our Life is brief:
The alarm, the struggle, the relief,
  Then sleep we side by side.

UNFADING hope! when life's last embers burn;
  When soul to soul, and dust to dust return, —
Heaven to thy charge resigns the awful hour:
Oh, then thy kingdom comes, immortal Power!
What though each spark of earth-born rapture fly
The quivering lip, pale cheek, and closing eye,
Bright to the soul thy seraph hands convey
The morning dream of life's eternal day.

WE feel our immortality o'ersweep
  All pain, all time, all tears, all fears, and peal
Like the eternal thunder of the deep
Into our ears this truth, — thou liv'st forever.

### 1.

DEATH hath made no breach
    In love and sympathy, in hope and trust.
No outward sigh or sound our ears can reach;
But there's an inward, spiritual speech
    That greets us still, though mortal tongues be dust.

### 2.

It bids us do the work that they laid down,
    Take up the song where they broke off the strain;
So journeying till we reach the heavenly town,
Where are laid up our treasures and our crown,
    And our lost loved ones will be found again.

---

NOT to the grave, not to the grave, my soul,
    Follow thy friend beloved!
But in the lonely hour,
But in the evening walk,
Think that he companies thy solitude;
Think that he holds with thee
Mysterious intercourse;
And, though remembrance wake a tear,
There will be joy in grief.

## DEATH OF THE YOUNG.

OH! it is hard to take
    The lesson that such deaths will teach.
But let no man reject it;
    For it is one that all must learn:
And it is a mighty, universal truth,
When death strikes down the innocent and young.
For every fragile form from which he lets
    The parting spirit free,
    A hundred virtues rise,
In shapes of mercy, charity, and love,
    To walk the world and bless it.
    Of every tear
That sorrowing mortals shed on such green graves,
Some good is born, some gentler nature comes.

## THE SPIRIT WORLD.

THE spirit land is real and substantial. Through every cycle of change that matter passes, some portions reach a higher state. There is no law of retrogression. Fragrance flows from blossoms: so spiritual elements constantly stream from the material world. The refined spiritual essences from this and other planetary worlds ascending into those vast ether regions, condense and gravitate, like purpling clouds fringed with gold, to their appropriate positions. These silver-edged strata, as arching zones stretching along the measureless blue above us, are too magnificent for description. Angels alone can tell their grandeur.

The spirit land, constituted, then, of the particles and etherealized essences from the many earths and systems that dot the universe, *all* bathed in the magnetic sunlight of an eternal morning, is no shadowy realm, but real and permanent, — "a city that hath foundation, whose maker and builder is God." There are forests, fields, mountains, valleys, groves, gardens, fruits, flowers, sparkling fountains, flowing rivers, pleasant grottoes; palatial mansions with gorgeous domes, constellated and astral; cottages and princely palaces with tesselated floors, tapestried walls and diamond-pointed ceilings. Over the portals of each holy habitation is inscribed Purity. Spirits residing within these angelic homes begin to fathom the riches of true love, — *love* such as glowed in the soul of John when he leaned upon the bosom of Jesus.

> "It is perpetual summer there. But here
> Sadly we may remember rivers clear,
> And harebells quivering on the meadow-floor.
> For brighter bells and bluer,
> For tenderer hearts and truer,
> People that happy land, the realm
>     Of Evermore."

As souls advance, their ideas expand. Progress is an eternal law. The universe is infinite. The ideal beckoning the real to "come up higher," there will ever be loftier, diviner altitudes to attain.

The inhabitants peopling the heavenly abodes of the hereafter, having passed through the disciplines of earth and the schoolings pertaining to the spirit-spheres, are earnest and untiring in their spiritual activities. Remembering their lives on earth, deep and holy are their sympathies for humanity. Love never forgets. In the morning-time and the gray of evening, down golden-tided rivers sail these ministering spirits of God to catch the incense of each soul-felt prayer. They come to impress and inspire. Their magnetisms are baptisms, their words the spirit-echoes of eternal life.

None say, in the Summer-Land of spirit-life, "I tread the wine-press alone." The law of harmonial associations is there fully realized. Those receptions of infants by matronly bands; those schools of tenderest discipline; those homes of mutual love embowered in roses; those palaces of art tinged with electric light; those cities of scientists, brotherhoods of philanthropists, and congresses of angels, — *all* add to the beatific glories of life in the republics of heaven. Those gifted with open vision, catching glimpses of landscapes and surpassingly beautiful scenery, often listen to the converse of immortals.

There are multitudes of dwellers in the spirit-world who are not properly in the spiritual world. Only the pure, the beautiful, and the spiritually-minded are in the spiritual world. These are they "that have overcome." Beyond them gladden the glories of celestial life.

Heaven is a condition of self-balance, harmony, and happiness. Depending more upon subjective relations than local surroundings, it is attained in all worlds only through aspiration and obedience to divine laws.

---

## *PRACTICAL SUGGESTIONS.*

HAVE the assembly-room neat and orderly at every session: a filthy and disordered hall breeds filthy morals. If possible, adorn the walls with pictures, significant mottoes, and other symbols of truth. Flowers are wonderfully cheering and beautiful: bring them in their season.

By practical example, teach the beautiful rules of courtesy: good manners are the blossom of good sense.

Let parents and guardians encourage the Lyceum by their presence at each session, and by taking part in the exercises. No person can be a dutiful Lyceum member and not grow in wisdom and in love. Expansion is for all, eternally.

Have the school well drilled in music. During the singing exercises, stand erect, holding your book nearly horizontal in front of the breast, low enough so that if it were raised to perpendicular it would not quite touch the chin; take the same position for reading.

Instruct the members in deep breathing: it is impossible to sing or read with good effect, unless the lungs are amply supplied with air; replenish them when the *pauses* occur.

Do not fear precision in your department: it is more conducive to grace than a slip-shod, careless manner. In going to the rostrum to read or recite, go quietly, but with alacrity; not as though you were in torture, and made your offering grudgingly: such a deportment will mar the pleasure of your listeners. Be glad to do what you can, and show this feeling in your face. Do not forget a respectful bow to your audience.

It is well for the younger groups to commit to memory and repeat moral maxims occasionally, or, if thought desirable, at every session.

Procure, if possible, special instructors occasionally to lecture, using designs, &c. A READING by a good artist will stimulate talent wonderfully, and be thus useful.

Bring cultivated SINGERS before your Lyceum now and then. A good concert is one of the most enjoyable and elevating entertainments, and by a little painstaking can be furnished.

Cultivate the dramatic: make the Lyceum the theatre of whatever ennobles the character. Spiritual dramas are both appropriate and refining on Sunday evenings. Rightly managed, this essential feature in the Lyceum system may be not only a source of financial revenue, but of reform.

An entertainment worth paying for, and sure to win patronage, almost any Lyceum may give if willing to work. It may consist of short dramas, tableaux, recitations, music, charades, and a few Lyceum exercises. Those invaluable friends of the Lyceum, Mr. and Mrs. Dyott, of Philadelphia, have used a very beautiful march for such occasions, called the "The March of the Angels." It is performed by thirty girls dressed in white, ornamented with gauze, flowers, &c.; the manner and changes in the marching can be arranged to suit the hall. They may march around it, and over the rostrum if there is sufficient room, performing various pleasing variations. Calisthenics in pretty costumes are fine, performed at exhibitions.

Nothing is more exhilarating to the little folks than a picnic. Do not forget that fact, when the summer is abroad with her verdure, flowers, and bird-music.

If you hold "Children's Sociables," go with your little ones, and see that they are home and in bed by ten o'clock. They cannot endure what older people can: all intellectual attainments are of little worth if health is ruined. We do not think children should dance often, or long at a time.

Never get discouraged at cruel words from those who are not of your belief. Have faith in truth, and remember that all cannot see alike. If any one should be unkind to you, you cannot afford to return it to him, since every sinful action stains your life.

---

## PARLIAMENTARY RULES.

### COMPILED BY HUDSON TUTTLE.

THE conductor, as the presiding officer during the sessions and official meetings of the Lyceum, is governed by parliamentary rules. A summary of the most essential usages is here inserted, compiled from authentic sources. These rules have been adopted because experience has taught their value, and should not, under any circumstances, be departed from. By adhering strictly to them, the association not only learns the rules maintained in all public bodies, — an important and useful lesson, — but order and regularity are preserved as they can be in no other manner.

The duty of the presiding officer is to preserve order, present the business of the meeting if not otherwise introduced, recognize the speakers, and put all properly-seconded motions to vote.

When any member means to speak, he is to stand up in his place, and address the presiding officer, who calls him by his name.

When a member stands up to speak, no question is to be put, but he is to be heard unless the assembly overrule him.

When two or more arise, the presiding officer recognizes the first, and the others must sit down. They may appeal to the assembly.

When the chairman arises to speak, all members should sit down. No one is to disturb another in his speech, by hissing, coughing, spitting, speaking, whispering, moving, or walking across the floor.

But should a speaker find, by the general indulgence of his auditors in such incivilities, that they do not wish to hear him, it is his duty to sit down.

No person, in speaking, should speak of another who is present, by name.

If repeated calls do not produce order, the chairman calls the offender or offenders by name. The assembly may then require his withdrawal. He is then to be heard in exculpation, and is to withdraw.

No person can be present when any business concerning himself is debating.

A question of order may be adjourned to give time to look into precedents.

The only case when a member has a right to insist on any thing, is when he calls for the execution of the order of the assembly. It is the duty of the chairman to carry this into execution.

When such order is made to transpire at a certain day, when the time arrives a question is to be put, when it is called for, whether the assembly is ready to proceed with the matter.

Orders of the day may be discharged at any time, and a new one made for a different day.

No motion shall be debated before seconded.

A motion must be re-stated by the chair as often as a member demands.

A motion cannot be withdrawn without the consent of the assembly.

No motion can be made without rising and addressing the chair.

When a question is under debate, no motion shall be received but to adjourn, to lay on the table, to postpone indefinitely, to postpone to a day certain, to commit, to amend; which several motions shall have precedence in the order they stand arranged, and the motion for adjournment shall always be in order, and decided without debate.

Motion to adjourn cannot be received after another question is actually put, and while the assembly is engaged in voting.

These questions are subject to the common principle, "first moved, first put," except when, amendment and postponement competing, the last is first put; and amendment and commitment, commitment must be put first.

The previous question is not allowed after motion to postpone, commit, or amend the main question.

The previous question cannot be amended.

An amendment may be moved to an amendment, but not in a higher degree.

When a blank is to be filled with a sum, or with a certain duration of time, the largest sum and longest time must be put first.

When a motion to strike out or agree to a paragraph has been made, motions to amend are to be put first, before a vote is taken on striking out or agreeing to.

A question of order arising out of any other question, or a matter of privilege, reading papers relative to the subject under discussion, or leave to withdraw a motion, must be put before the principal question.

When any question is before the assembly, any member may move the previous question, " Whether that question (called the main question) shall now be put?" If it pass in the affirmative, then the main question is to be put immediately; and no man may speak any thing further to it, either to add or alter.

On an amendment being moved, a member who has spoken to the main question may speak again to the amendment.

Amendments may be made so as totally to alter the nature of the proposition.

Tellers of votes are appointed by the chair.

No one can vote after the decision is announced by the chair.

While the assembly is telling, no member may speak or move out of his place.

A motion to adjourn, simply, cannot be amended; but must be put simply "that the —— do now adjourn.

# APPENDIX.

## OPINIONS OF CONDUCTORS OF LYCEUMS AND OLD FRIENDS OF THE INSTITUTION.

WISHING to present in this work the experience of our Lyceums up to the present time, that we may be profited by each others' practical wisdom, we published in the spiritual papers a circular, addressed to Conductors and other Lyceum friends, soliciting answers to the following questions, which called out a generous response from all sections of the country. We assure our correspondents of our gratitude for their whole-souled co-operation. We publish all our space will allow, and regret that we are compelled to leave any letters unpublished.

While we have aimed at order and system in the present work, we have avoided the stultifying monotony of formalities. We do not advise *stereotyped methods*. What we have done is suggestive, not final. We have merely erected an industrial building, with machinery and tools in it; and we trust that the architects of mind will use this with a constant effort to devise new and improved means of education, not as we fancy, but as to them is wise and practical. Work, *head*-work, is absolutely necessary to success in this direction. The following letters will aid, in many ways, all studious workers:—

### THE PUBLISHED QUESTIONS.

1. In what moral estimate do you reckon the Lyceum system as superior to the Church Sunday school?
2. What facts, or incidents, can you relate, of your Lyceum, demonstrative of such superiority?
3. Has your Lyceum been instrumental in developing the mediumistic powers of the youth?
4. What methods have you found most successful in securing habits of punctuality with the members of your Lyceum?
5. What are the best means of obtaining the co-operation of parents and guardians, and their frequent attendance upon the sessions of the Lyceum?
6. What is your opinion of making our Lyceums more dramatic?
7. What are the best methods of securing finances for the support of the Lyceum?
8. Do you favor the one-lecture system, that more time may be given to the interests of the Lyceum?

# APPENDIX.

9. Will you please state what otherwise you regard as advantageous to the improvement and progress of our work of love?

*From Stanley H. A. Frisbie, Brooklyn, N. Y.*

In answer to your questions, I send the following brief response: —
1. By expanding the mind instead of cramping it.
2. Brightness of intellect and happiness of spirit.
3. It has.
4. Encouragement, with discipline of a moral nature.
5. Getting their good will by frequent communion.
6. By introducing the drama, but I do not think it advances.
7. A certain amount paid per month, always in advance.
9. Circulate tracts, books; have public exhibitions, meetings, picnics, and parades.

---

*From Nath. Randall, M.D., Woodstock, Vt.*

It seems to me Lyceums are of more use to adults than to the young, at this time. We cannot afford to wait to train the youth alone; the older ones should be drilled for the hour. The battle is now the hardest. In the Southern rebellion, we wanted efficient officers in the outbreak; we could not wait for men to be trained years in a military school before they did any service. Neither can we now wait for the youth to mature in the Lyceum. Let old and young work and learn together.

---

*From Edwin Wilder, Hingham, Mass.*

I shall be able to give only a little experience in the conducting of a small Lyceum in this town. We have been in existence and holding a Lyceum regularly, without vacations or intermission, for three years. During the first year of our existence, we had regular speakers, once in two weeks, and at that time the Lyceum had members and friends, numbering some sixty. Our funds failing to keep the two organizations in running order, it was deemed the wisest and best course to sustain the Lyceum regularly through the year, and to have lectures only when in funds to allow it. Result, many professed thorough-going spiritualists dropped away, and went back to the church, where they could sit at ease and be talked into heaven. This, with the usual bickering about place and office, reduced our whole number of old and young down to forty, or a little less. For the lack of means we have had but three speakers the past year, preferring to keep the Lyceum in its work, and do in it what we may to develop our own faculties, and assist the children in taking their first steps up into broader views of life and duty, to being hearers only of the word. I know it is much easier to dress on Sunday and attend two lectures, than it is to prepare one's-self during the week for the Lyceum, and on Sunday take an active part in all the various exercises. In the latter, one has some work, some thinking, some acting to do. In the former he becomes a sponge to drink in, but never to give out without pressure; and, if never pressed, it remains to dry up and pass away, without use to itself or others. And this is the very reason we prefer to continue the Lyceum system to that of lectures, if but one can be sustained. At the end of the year, we have gained something; got something as a remainder. But if we spend the same amount of money for speakers we spend for Lyceum expenses one year, we could have six good speakers one day each, having, with the Lyceum, fifty-two meetings, when in the other case we should have twelve, and our children at some Sunday school.

Original thought, put into words, *written* or *spoken*, by every member of the Lyceum, is the crowning point over the usual Sunday school. To read, and to think for one's-self is what we want to make better men and women. When we become true to ourselves, we shall be true to others.

No mediumistic powers have been developed in whole or in part, to my knowledge, in our Lyceum.

Punctuality! what an awful word that is; what feelings it engenders to all, whichever side they belong! The only means I ever have used to produce the desired result is always, at all times, to *be there.*

To keep parents and friends interested, and constant in attendance, I have tried to read or say something, immediately after the opening exercises, general, and applying equally to all; sometimes change, and adapt it especially to the older ones, and then again to the very youngest.

I think dramatics well calculated to kindle the fire that otherwise would remain slumbering. Our Lyceum has experienced great trials in the musical department.

I have found great assistance in "The Lyceum Banner," both in music and silver-chain recitations, but not enough to relieve us from trouble. We have secured all the music published by Mrs. Lou. H. Kimball, and think it good.

---

*From A. G. Smith, Painesville, O.*

In response to your published wish for replies to questions concerning the management of Lyceums, a few brief words must tell our ideas: —
1. We hold the Lyceum to be superior to church Sunday schools, in that it inculcates mental expansion instead of stagnation.
2. This is evident in the life and growth of all.
4. Adhering to regular hours for Lyceum exercises.
5. Appoint them to places of trust, thereby making them feel they have a part to take, and must be at their post.
6. Our experience would say, not too much of the dramatic. Good in its place; develops in a certain direction; but may engross all other thought.
7. We are too poor to afford an answer; but may say, *Never* divorce the Society and Lyceum.
8. Yes; or if two, let the morning lecture be given during, or immediately after, the Lyceum session, and *in the interest* of its cause.
9. All work, and no time or excuse for petty jealousy. Conductors, we believe, might advantageously exchange suggestions as to methods, and perhaps "charges" (is that orthodox?).

We are glad to know that we are to have a new book for general use. We have felt its need.

# APPENDIX.

### From A. B. Randall, Appleton, Wis.

I think one lecture, or one sermon, per Sabbath, is quite enough, if good. If poor, two is certainly one too many. I prefer to die a natural death, to being preached or lectured to death: that is not an easy way to die. With us, funds are easiest collected by sending little juveniles through the hall during the Lyceum hour, especially to defray incidental expenses.

For other expenses, concerts, sociables, dances, oyster suppers, &c., where a fee is charged at the door, have worked well with us, and given general satisfaction. These need not interfere with subscriptions for building halls. &c., &c.

The great needs of the spiritualists, and most other liberals, are halls of their own. When a society has a hall, or temple, all the other matters follow naturally, such as lectures, Lyceum sociables, &c.; but when we have to pay an exorbitant price for a hall, or meet in some out-of-the-way or obscure place, the car drags heavily, and, in most cases, discouragingly.

### From E. Thompson, Ormo, Wis.

1. It leaves the mind free: instead of repeating authority, it teaches to be self-reliant, and to express an opinion without fear of conflicting with priesthood.
2. In learning to speak in public without embarrassment.
3. Not yet to be perceived, only in one way: it has caused children's circles to be held, where child spirits delight to come and talk with them. Children are very much profited and interested in such circles.
4. If tardy, not allowed to wear badges; awarding prizes for punctuality, good behavior, declamations, and answering questions.
5. In keeping good order, making the Lyceum interesting, respecting all alike, and seeking to prevent aspiration for position.
6. Think it a good plan, but always to confine it to the members of the Lyceum.
7. Not in favor of having entertainments so often as to weary the patience of the people; but watch your opportunity, and have one occasionally at the right time. Deficiency in money should be made up by subscription.
8. Yes.
9. The world can never be converted as it is: it must be changed by the rising generation.

### From Abel L. Butterworth, East Franklin, N.H.

The suggestion I wish to offer for Children's Lyceums, or, in fact, for any elevating entertainment, is this:—

Take a short poem (or a prose piece) like Coleridge's "Love, Hope, and Patience in Education," and let there be three girls dressed in white, pretty near the same size, and a boy to repeat the poem, one with a good, clear, flexible voice, who understands something of rhythm. Let the girls form a tableau, as described in the poem, at the point beginning,

"Methinks I see them grouped in seemly show
The straightened arms upraised, the palms aslope;
And robes that, touching as adown they flow,
Distinctly blend like snow embossed in snow."

Before raising the curtain, let the dresses be arranged, in order to comply with the language of the poem; and as each description turns, as in the line,

"And bending o'er with soul-transfusing eyes,
And the soft murmurs of the mother dove."

As this part is reached, let Love bend over towards Hope, who seems to have yielded a little, and carry ont the idea given in the lines above; and so on through the poem, till at the close, the whole labor of Patience can be shown by Love and Hope seeming to rest heavily on Patience, by clasping their arms around her neck, she still retaining her position of "*the arms upraised, the palms aslope,*" as if still upbearing the burden as well as the other two. When the boy repeating the poem slowly, yet very distinctly, comes to the words, "Yet haply there will come a *weary day,*" let him, as well as possible, dwell on the word weary, so as to show the full beauty of the steady endurance of Patience, and the value of the principle.

I think if this could be thoroughly introduced, it would add considerably to the beauty of an entertainment, and make a combination of Tableau and Recitation that could not fail to please; but in selecting, choose only short pieces, so as not to try the endurance of the personators of the tableau too far.

### From S. W. Foster, A. B. Plympton, and others, Lowell, Mass.

In answering the questions of the circular enclosed, I do so as best I may, in accordance with the various opinions of many of the leading minds, and the best friends of the Lyceum, whom I have consulted in our city. I have thought this a better way than to give barely my own views.
1. Superior in the method of natural unfoldment, as opposed to supernatural.
2. It leaves the child, or person, in possession of reason, and the natural faculties of observation.
3. The Lyceum system tends to make positive the natural action of the mental and spiritual faculties, thereby destroying the necessary conditions for foreign mediumship. The Orthodox Sabbath Schools are the best medium nurseries, where its victims, taught to be nothing themselves, make the best subjects for the control of others, both in and out of the flesh.
4. Questions that are interesting, *comprehensive*, and appropriate to the different groups, and tact and taste on the part of the leaders to fasten the attention of the pupils upon the subject to be considered.
5. Lecture in the forenoon, Lyceum session to follow; and let the people be most earnestly implored to bring their children to *both*. We are in favor of very short Lectures, the most of us; and we think that two hours for the Lyceum session is as much time as can be profitably occupied.
6. No doubt the dramatic element is somewhat useful; but there is great danger of misusing it, to the extent of creating a *sensational* condition.
7. One of the best methods of raising funds, &c., is to so educate all those who may be, and are, interested in progression, up to the idea that it is their *duty* to contribute towards the support of the Lyceum. Concerts, exhibitions, &c., we find are very useful to this end. Another way to raise funds is to raise more friends and less enemies;

and the best way to do this, especially since so many of our *tall* radicals have such *short* purses as to be *useless* to us, is *not* to be so near like them ourselves; we may find friends, *use,* and *money* among the more conservative and practical element of society.

8. Most of the spiritualists of Lowell are not in favor of the one-lecture system. When spiritualists, or others, desire to attend a lecture, let them have access to the best sort the world affords.

*From G. W. Kates, Cincinnati, Ohio.*

I cannot refrain from expressing my views in reference to your Lyceum Guide, because I deem it highly necessary that it be published.

The manual of A. J. Davis is good — *exceedingly good*— so far as it goes; but the demand of the Lyceum is for greater variety. Manuals and guides may be issued in voluminous form, or in great numbers, yet the demands of the Lyceum will be for more; still the Lyceums will be leaving the pathways of thought and action marked out by the gifted and intelligent minds that have been their authors, and will develop for themselves exercises, rules, and regulations; in fact, they will use their own faculties and inspirations in all the departments of their beloved movement. This freedom and self-sovereignty is the greatest beauty of the system. I wish you assistance from all our Lyceums and the spirit-world, in producing as thorough a guide as possible.

I will endeavor to briefly notice your questions.

1. I claim that the Lyceum is superior to the church Sunday school in moral influence, as follows: In teaching that our lives in all their beauty and happiness, here and hereafter, are dependent on our actions in accordance with our highest conceptions of truth. In teaching that our relatives, friends, and other loving souls gone on to the summer-land, are actually present, ministering spirits to our souls and their needs.

In discarding all myths as absolute word of God, receiving them as thoughts to be weighed for their practised worth. Recognizing God as a perfect principle, instead of a personified being; and " the word of God" as being *all truths wherever found.*

I observed that the members of our Lyceums more generally desire and love to attend than Sunday-school scholars do.

3. Cultivate the aspirations towards the true, the beautiful, and the good, and mediumistic powers will be unfolded. I believe the Lyceum has greater opportunities in this direction than most circles.

To produce mediumship, culture must be given the body, mind, and soul of the young. Early seed must be sown, which will produce in the future man or woman true manhood and womanhood, parents of perfect children; hence mediums. Cultivation is the lever upon which rests the grandest possibilities of the future medium.

4. To commence the exercises promptly at a given hour, whether few or many are present.

5. More earnest work on the part of officers and leaders in the Lyceum and out of it. Leaders, by visiting the homes of their scholars, will find the result good. More diversity in the exercises. Invite any person present to speak on the question.

6. I am in favor of cultivating the dramatic talent of our Lyceums. I think every one should have a dramatic club, and in exhibitions, short dramas should be produced.

7. I believe our Lyceums should always control their own finances. To get finances, means to work. By subscriptions, collections, and exhibitions, Lyceums should and will thrive, if energetically managed.

8. I think two lectures are, in the present condition of our societies, in most cases necessary. The conference meeting in connection with the Lyceum, by having the lecturer lead, would perhaps be an improvement where lecturers have extended engagements.

9. This is an inexhaustible question. The special demand is for more earnest workers, and more attention to, and recognition of, the importance of the Lyceum. It is impossible to see to-day the grand possibilities of the future; but there is one thing of which I feel certain; that is, the Lyceum is to be one of the grandest means of public benefit to the youth that has ever been inaugurated. It is also the best and most practical method of building a sure foundation for the grand superstructure of spiritualism.

*From Hudson Tuttle, Milan, O.*

The Lyceum, of which the great spiritual and rationalistic movements are a part, is diametrically opposed to the old and received methods of thought. The old has ever sought to force man to become perfected by means of foreign and external agencies; but this seeks the object by means of internal growth. Not in the past; not on cross, or in dungeon; not in moulding ashes of dead men, or moulding parchment of the dead ideas of dead men, — are we to seek for truths, but within ourselves, and the living present. There are no books that teach this knowledge. Tradition, the clinging to the old, dread of the new, all are against us. Our success depends entirely on individuals. On this account have I feared for the reformatory movement inaugurated by the Lyceum. It depends entirely on individual effort, and few are prepared to give the aid it demands. When efficient officers have taken hold of it, they have met success. Whenever they have neglected their duty, failure resulted.

It is no sinecure to conduct a Lyceum, to be guardian or leader. It means work, and as much as you please to give. If the officers are punctual, the children will be. The conductor should study, by various means, to make the sessions diversified and interesting. He should rule by love, and arbitrary authority, jealousy, envy, be kept from the hall of the Lyceum.

Dramatics should be cultivated, but not so as to weary the children or exhaust their energies.

The Lyceum is a growing institution; it is living. Forms and stereotyped sessions should be avoided. The field for expansion is as broad as the universe. I repeat what I consider the essential element of its success; efficient, thorough, self-sacrificing officers, who are willing to labor earnestly and indefatigably. Having them, triumph is certain; without them, failure is inevitable.

*From Horace Dresser, D.D.*

In getting up your book, pray be so kind as to accommodate it to Spiritualism as a religion, not a

philosophy merely. It should aim especially to arouse and cultivate the emotional, the devotional elements of our nature. In a Lyceum, intellectual culture should be secondary; it is chiefly cared for in the other schools. To this end, the poetry and music, if inspiring, will be grand instrumentalities.
. . . Try to reform the pronunciation of *Lyceum*. Why will persons pronounce it Ly-cē-um instead of Ly-cĕ-um, as it should be on account of its Greek derivation? . . . Let the Lyceum be an institution in which children shall receive moral and religious culture under the auspices of Spiritualism and its cognate instrumentalities, and I can then bid it God-speed. I think your book will be adapted to such high object. With such improvements as your taste and judgment abundantly qualify you to make, the Lyceums will become centres of public interest and attraction.

*From J. S. Loveland, San Francisco, Cal.*

Those who educate a nation's children shape its destiny. No class are more thoroughly awake to this fact than the clergy, and hence the untiring assiduity with which they labor to keep the educational appliances in their own hands. We ought to be able to see as clearly as they do, and work as zealously for the true as they toil for the false. In every city, village, and town, we ought to form ourselves into schools or lyceums, not of the children only, but of all, old and young. Libraries should be collected, scientific apparatus procured, and a course of study at once entered upon. Lectures of instruction would be given; and we should very soon find ourselves in the full tide of successful experiment, with the great world following hard after us.

*From John B. Wolff, Washington, D.C.*

You ask for facts and opinions: —
1. The superiority of the Lyceum is exhibited in the fact that it is self-educating; that it unfetters and draws out, instead of fettering and driving in; 2, In combining physical and mental culture; 3, In the mode of that culture, producing *unity* of *action*, *unity* of *thought*, harmonious development, a grand army of progress keeping time with the internal forces of Mother Nature and Father God.
2. The black-board and object-teaching in the winter; 2, Outdoor teaching from natural objects, on summer Sundays when the weather is fair.
3. Music. Here we fail with adults and children. We need congregational singing and Lyceum singing. The latter is better provided than the former. But what we need most is a system of musical notation, simple, easily understood, and adapted to old and young. Such a system I have; a child ten years old can learn and understand it in a few hours, and thenceforward read music in this system the same as common composition, whenever and wherever found. I want spiritualism to have the first use of this, if possible.

*From Harvey A. Jones, Sycamore, Ill.*

I gladly add my testimony in favor of the Progressive Lyceum system. It is as much an improvement on the old Sunday-school routine as the rationalistic and inspirational spirit of the Harmonial Philosophy is in advance of the creed-bound religions of our century.
1. One of the best fruits of the system is, that it makes workers of even the youngest children; they feel that its various exercises are *theirs*. They are led to seek and find truth. And the lesson of self-redemption is in the physical as well as the mental and moral training.
2. The receptive and earnest mind, thus cultivated, conduces to inspirational powers and the various phases of mediumship for the highest influences.
3. The responsibility of equal shares in labor, and mutual interests and reciprocal aid, are the strongest ties that can bind together a band of workers. One feature or innovation that is now extensively adopted in other Lyceums, in which strangers and visitors readily join, originated, I believe, with our Lyceum in Sycamore. Instead of the "Answer to General Question," the giving of some sentiment or proverb, — a word of wisdom we term it. — either original or selected; and we have made it one of the most lively and interesting parts of our exercises. This change, suggested by Mrs. Jones, and reported at the Lyceum Convention that was holden at Chicago, in conjunction with the State Spiritualist Convention, in June, 1868, has become a Lyceum feature, and some Orthodox Sunday schools even, in this vicinity, have adopted it with some modifications.
4. All the variety practicable with your material should be given in the exercises, to awaken and hold interest. Dramatic exercises could come in here as an aid. Of course, this takes a large margin of time and energy, which Lyceum workers have not always at command.
5. In our three years' experience, we have found it better that a Lyceum be self-supporting, at least for all ordinary expenses. Weekly re-unions or sociables of the younger members at private homes, with a small voluntary donation for this purpose, has worked the best with us. We organized three years since (come July), under the auspices of Dr. S. J. Avery of Chicago Lyceum, our noble and generous sponsor, with but three resident families of spiritualists who had small children; of these three families, two have removed to a distance, and no new-comers from abroad have replaced them. Of course, we have made some working material, and bad other help; but the main prop of a Lyceum — children — are now and have been wanting since the first three months, when the novelty subsided, and opposition could concentrate its forces.
6. Undoubtedly the Lyceum should be the paramount interest in our liberal organizations, above any lecture system; for from the Lyceum we must expect its future recruits and workers. The young should be our first care. The fortifications of error are not always taken and *held* by storm; the quiet but *persistent* influence of truth permeates and transforms till better things take the place of the old.

*From Albert Stegeman, Allegan, Mich.*

To raise finances we take up the "free-gifts" that are brought by the members of, and the visitors to, our Lyceums each Sunday; and during the winter we have held social dances once a week, from six to nine, P.M., charging an admittance fee of fifty cents per couple for outsiders, and ten cents each for our own members. Besides this, we have a subscription paper signed by as many of our number as feel able to give, payable quarterly in advance. We are nine months old, and have our outfit paid for, and have money in our treasury.

We must wake up spiritualists to the importance of our *work*, and cause them to feel (if possible) that it is *our* work, and not leave it for the angel world to do.

Many who have joined our ranks are persons who for years have been idlers, standing aloof from the changes going on in the world of mind; having no longer fear of a Devil to overtake them, nor a hell awaiting them, they seem content to float along like drift-wood, saying "It is all right."

### From Dr. C. C. York, Charlestown, Mass.

I found, when conductor some three years since, the best way to interest children was to have four kinds of tickets, one for *punctual attendance*, another *group answers*, another *good behavior*, another *good speaking*.

When the Lyceum was called to order, the guardian and assistants went around to each group and gave a ticket to each scholar present, and marked it to the scholar; when the questions were asked of the groups, the guardian and assistants would give each scholar who answered a ticket; when called to speak, those who spoke well received a ticket; the last service was for the guardian and her assistants to ask the leaders who had been good scholars, and give such a ticket.

We had so many to speak that we were obliged to have the girls one Sunday, and boys the next. All behaved well, all answered questions, nearly all were in their seats when called to order. We had some eighty constant members. It was interesting.

When the four youngest groups had a certain number of tickets, we received them, and gave a reward of merit; and so with all. It was a great amount of work; but it paid well in the interest it created, and the progress the children made.

We formed a sewing-circle to work, not to gossip in; and all the poor children we could influence to come we gave some clothing, and in a few cases gave the child an entire suit; and by being kind, and myself visiting every child's parent or guardian, and becoming well acquainted with them, I was pretty sure to have their company in the Lyceum Sunday.

If we wished an entertainment, we could very easily have one, and make a handsome sum for the good of the children.

I think it best to make the Lyceum as dramatic as possible, but not overtax the young.

In most all Lyceums, the time spent for instructing the children is not more than half as long as it should be.

My aim was to act so every child could love me. I can see its fruits to-day; and oh what will it be in spirit-life!

---

### From George D. Gleason, Philadelphia.

Having labored in the Lyceum cause for the last six years, I send my offering.

1st. I consider the Lyceum system superior to the Church Sunday school because the lessons are addressed to the reason of the children, instead of to their fears, and because morality and common sense are inculcated instead of superstition and bigotry. Early impressions are the most lasting, and training should begin in the right direction.

2d. I could relate several, but let one suffice. On the occasion of our last picnic, there was a bird's nest on a small tree near the dancing platform. The limb which supported the nest was within reach of any boy twelve years old; and although, during the afternoon, I saw several boys pull down the limb, and look at the three eggs in the nest, when the company left for home the little structure was still unharmed.

3d. I am not aware that it has.

4th. We have had little delinquency with the children. I think we never should have any if our officers and leaders were punctual; but too often they are not present at the hour for commencing the session. We have had the musical director instruct the children in singing, half an hour before opening, and have found the effect good.

5th. We have not had regular attendance from parents; many never attend at all; some appear indifferent whether their children go or not; but all cooperate with us in our exhibitions, selling tickets, &c.

6th. If you mean to have a *Dramatic Association* formed by the members of the Lyceum, I am not in favor of it, as I think it would produce jealousy and inharmony, besides being a great expense. I think it would not show off the talent of the members as well as an annual or semi-annual Exhibition.

7th. Make the sessions as attractive as possible, and take up a collection at every one. Try and induce your friends to visit the Lyceum, particularly on *Convention days*; explain the system to strangers, and be civil, if you cannot be polite, to all visitors. When you give Exhibitions, sell tickets, if you can, to your sectarian brothers and sisters who are less fortunate than you in understanding the beauties of our religion; be careful not to wound their feelings, or mar the beauty of a speech by heartless and cruel epithets hurled at those who are yet in the churches.

8th. I do; but in most places it is a hard change to inaugurate, and I fear would detract from the meagre support even now given to the societies. Grown people are afraid of "being cheated" on one lecture a Sunday.

In regard to improvements, I would suggest furnishing each member with a copy of the Lyceum Banner, published by Mrs. Lou Kimball of Chicago. Have a good library and a competent librarian. We have in our collection of books all the spiritual works, a Scientific and Religious Department, but find travels and novels are most sought after.

Every Lyceum should have a catalogue of its books. My system for collecting and delivering books is this: the assistant librarian or one of the guards hands the leader of each group a leather strap, like an old-fashioned skate-strap, having the name and number of the group marked on it; the pupil has a number from the catalogue written on a card or paper, to which his or her name and name of group is added, and this is placed inside of the book to be returned. The books are given to the leader, who places them all together, and buckles the strap around them. This done, the officer for that duty takes these all to the library, takes off the strap, keeping the lists of each group and the straps together. After the returned books are placed on the shelves, the guards or librarians each take one list and select a book from it, place the list in the book, and the book on the strap of "Liberty Group," for instance; so doing until all the books are chosen for that group, and the strap is buckled around them. So proceed until all the straps are filled, when the officers deliver the packets to the leaders, who distribute to their members, and return the strap to the officers, to be placed in the library or banner-chest. This plan worked

# APPENDIX.

well when our Lyceum was three hundred strong, entirely obviating all confusion.

I think giving little presents for good behavior, a badge, book, or pin, if the latter could be furnished for fifty, would be encouraging.

Temperance and anti-tobacco pledges I approve, but think children should not be over-persuaded to sign them. A brief lecture, now and then, on temperance, morality, tobacco, the laws of health, &c., will do good.

There is a form of salute given by Mr. Davis for Lyceum members which I think much of: place the left hand on the heart, palm outward, fingers pointing upward; then let the hand fall naturally down by the side. The meaning of this is: "I SHOW THE ANGELS THE FACE OF MY HEART."

This is very pretty for closing the session. The conductor counts one, two, three, and at the word three, the whole Lyceum clap hands once, salute the conductor, and the conductor the members, by the described sign.

A Lyceum cannot afford to do without a good musical director, if obliged to pay fifty dollars a year to secure one.

Leaders' meetings should be held at least once a month, and all business talked over there, so that nothing disturbing need enter the Lyceum room. Never allow electioneering, or any thing approaching it, in the hall. When you see a person trying to move heaven and earth for an office, you may safely conclude that he would make you trouble if elected.

A society for looking after the needs of poor children in the Lyceum, whose parents have become suddenly unfortunate, or have been removed by death, may do much good; but to gather in the children from alleys and lanes,— beggars, bootblacks, news-boys, &c., — sometimes brings more evil influence into an assembly than the good brought to bear on *them* can overbalance. But let us be democratic, and do all the good we can.

---

*From S. B. Fairchild, St. Louis, Mo.*

Noticing your request, that conductors and friends of the Lyceum movement would answer certain inquiries, I submit the following as the result of my experience.

1. I regard it as greatly superior, in that it develops, in a natural way, the spiritual perceptions.

2. We have many instances, in this Lyceum, where children from other Sunday schools have come among us, their first answers to questions being strictly parrot-like, taken from the Bible, or their Sunday-school books; but, after a few Sundays, they would seem to have started in new avenues of thought, their soul-freedom being marked by the most progressive ideas.

4. The method we are using here now is the best we have had. That is: The leaders call the roll of their groups immediately after the Lyceum assembles, and those not present to answer to their names have a credit deducted from them; and, as our credits all have a *money value*, it becomes the *interest* of each child to be promptly in attendance. We have always been strictly honest and prompt in the faithful distribution of presents on each anniversary; and the children have the utmost confidence that they will receive, according to their merits, whatever has been promised them. As we are all, old and young, governed, in this winter-land, by selfishness, it is well to put that motive power in operation in securing good attendance; and we do it.

5. We find that the parents of children will come to the Lyceum when *their* children are to take some prominent or active part in the exercises.

Our convention-day exercises, once a month, when each child is urged to undertake some rostrum exercise, invariably attract large audiences. It has been a great feature in the success of this Lyceum.

6. I regard it as very important, to stimulate and promote the growth of this branch of the Lyceum system.

7. This subject has ever been, with us, a difficult one. We have always labored under pecuniary hardship. At present, we exist by private donations of the older members of the Lyceum and their friends. Our collection on convention day assists us very much. We have sociables twice a month, which more than pay expenses. I cannot suggest a "*best* method" for procuring finances.

8. The one-lecture system has been the rule here for over a year, and works well.

I regard the office of Musical Director of the utmost importance; and it is necessary that this officer should be not only competent, but enthusiastic and willing in the discharge of the duties of the position. A sociable feeling is very necessary to the success of a Lyceum. There should be frequent gatherings at the houses of officers and leaders.

---

*From D. N. Ford, Boston, Mass.*

In the "American Spiritualist" of Feb. 26, I find an article to conductors and other friends of the "Children's Progressive Lyceum." I am rejoiced to know that a new Lyceum book is so nearly completed; for I, with others, have felt the necessity of such a work.

Having been connected with the First Boston Lyceum since its organization, and its conductor for nearly two years, I think I know something of our shortcomings, if I cannot point out a remedy. We need the zeal which they manifest, whom we look down upon, in Sectarian Sunday schools. We may work never so hard to dazzle the eyes of the people; but, if we have not the true spiritual element in our work, our institution will be a short-lived one. Our intentions are undoubtedly good; but, as innovators, we must have a strong basis of principle to build upon. We know that our principles are elevating, and what we want is harmonious work, individual and in concert. We need not facts to prove that every act of life exerts an influence upon ourselves and those about us for good or evil.

Our Lyceum has been instrumental in developing mediumistic power. A number, since joining us, have been developed, and are now in the lecture-field. Question Number Four I would like to answer differently than to say we have not been eminently successful in securing habits of punctuality. We, however, are not behind other Lyceums in that respect. There are some people in whom the disease is chronic, *always behind time*. The trouble is generally with the adults, not the children.

To obtain the co-operation of parents and guardians requires us to interest the children, make our light so shine that the little ones who cluster about us, Sunday after Sunday, will carry that light to their homes. Leaders must, of course, visit those homes, show their faces to the parents and guardians, and by kind words prove that they are imbued with a spirit of love, and no contracted sectarian principle, causing the soul to shrink within its shell, saying, "Pure I, wicked you."

# APPENDIX.

It is our experience that too much of the dramatic is exhausting to the vitality which is necessary to the performance of strictly Lyceum work. True, it serves as an attraction; but those who engage in it are too apt to forget the simpler, yet far more necessary, duties they owe the spiritual Sunday school. The pecuniary profits from them have been very small. I think good Lyceum entertainments, which will bring out the talents of old and young, but especially the latter, are best calculated to create a healthy interest. The great want stares me in the face, viz., efficient leaders. If we can draw into that little circle of love those who can interest children, and who truly love the little buds of humanity, whose warm, sweet natures are pictured in their faces, then we need not fear that the Lyceum will be any thing but a success. We should instil into their minds healthy, natural ideas of God in man, the duties we owe to each other, and that every act of our lives will inevitably be followed by a result which will be happiness or sorrow to ourselves or others, and that the blood and tears of ten thousand Christs cannot wash away one square inch of stain from the garments of the evil-doer.

*From Olive Stevens, East Toledo, O.*

I send the following in reply to your questions:—
The Lyceum teaches that it is better to cultivate and expand our own thoughts than to learn and repeat the thoughts of others; that it is better to advance into the broad fields of science than to be cramped up in narrow theologies; that, instead of teaching the young to be idle and do no work on every seventh day, it teaches that our happiness is increased by working at least one day in seven for the improvement of our minds. The calisthenic exercises are useful to develop concentration of thought as well as grace. The harmony of music, thought, and motion has a tendency to inspire feelings of love for the order and harmony of nature.

*From J. A. Unthonk, Belle Creek, Nebraska.*

I wish to make a remark in regard to the selections of silver-chain recitations. Old Orthodoxy has sung of heaven these many years, but has failed to fill its measure in this; now, let us not fall into the same error. While we believe, and teach, and *know*, of a summer land, let our main thoughts and strength be devoted to perfecting ourselves in this. We are in eternity *to-day*; and if we are continually looking forward to the future, and contemplating the glories of the Summer Land, it is possible we may fail to drive the winter from this.

# INDEX.

## MUSIC.

| | PAGE. | | PAGE. |
|---|---|---|---|
| An Opening Song | 12 | Rest for the Weary | 58 |
| A Requiem | 32 | Star of the Evening | 5 |
| Are we not Brothers? | 53 | Speak, no Matter what Betide | 31 |
| Beautiful Angel | 54 | Sing All Together | 47 |
| Be Happy | 26 | The Beautiful Hills | 6 |
| Be Kind to Each Other | 51 | The Unseen City | 18 |
| Cherish Kindly Feelings | 9 | The Children | 20 |
| Closing Song | 13 | The Rock of Liberty | 21 |
| Come to the Woods | 16 | The Turf shall be my Fragrant Shrine | 23 |
| Christmas Bells | 24 | The Power of Little Things | 29 |
| Evergreen Mountains of Life | 46 | The Lyceum March | 34 |
| How I would Die | 22 | The World is growing Good | 40 |
| Hard Times come again No More | 59 | The Mountains of Life | 46 |
| I Live for Those who Love Me | 50 | The Promised Land To-morrow | 52 |
| Invocation to the Angels | 65 | The Old and the New | 56 |
| Keep a Pure Heart | 13 | The Golden Side | 57 |
| Let Us Love while we may | 10 | Truth | 64 |
| Life's Beautiful Sea | 36 | The Art of Beauty | 9 |
| Liberty's Army | 44 | The Angels of Consolation | 64 |
| Let us gather up the Sunbeams | 60 | The Night has gathered up her Moonlit Fringes | 65 |
| Meet us at the Crystal Gate | 14 | | |
| Morn amid the Mountains | 25 | Where have the Beautiful gone? | 38 |
| Marching Song | 30 | We shall meet our Friends in the Morning | 48 |
| Moonlight and Starlight | 42 | Work is Prayer | 61 |
| Onward and Sunward | 8 | We love the Father | 62 |
| Old " Glory Hallelujah " | 17 | Walk with the Beautiful | 64 |
| Oh! hear the Shout of the Brave ring out | 28 | Where the Roses ne'er shall wither | 27 |
| O Sacred Presence | 63 | Your Mission | 16 |

# INDEX.

## MUSICAL READINGS.

| | PAGE |
|---|---|
| Always a Future | 66 |
| The Angels | 67 |
| The Beautiful | 68 |
| In Knowledge there is Safety | 69 |
| Remember the Poor | 70 |
| Home Affections | 71 |
| Courage | 72 |
| Victory at Last | 73 |
| Scatter Roses | 74 |
| Glances Backward | 75 |
| Liberty and Reason | 76 |
| Childhood Morals | 77 |
| I Can't and I Can | 78 |
| Peace | 80 |
| The Hereafter | 80 |
| The Dawn of Redemption | 104 |
| The Beautiful Land | 106 |
| Trust to the Future | 108 |
| The Spirit World | 109 |
| The Voice of Progress | 111 |
| The World would be the Better for it | 121 |
| There must be Something Wrong | 121 |
| The World's Lie | 122 |
| The Inward Power | 123 |
| The Hymn of Night | 123 |
| There's no Dearth of Kindness | 128 |
| The Island of Long Ago | 128 |
| The Island of By and By | 130 |
| Voices | 97 |
| Voices of the Past and Future | 114 |
| When this old Earth is Righted | 96 |

## GOLDEN CHAIN RECITATIONS.

| | PAGE |
|---|---|
| A Ladder of Light | 96 |
| A Moral Code | 113 |
| Beatitudes | 83 |
| Better than Gold | 86 |
| Be Kind | 127 |
| Charity | 91 |
| Disappointments | 87 |
| Drop Charity's Curtain | 105 |
| Esteem Thyself | 98 |
| Flowers | 115 |
| God Reigns in the Earth | 85 |
| God is Forever with Man | 131 |
| Hope On, Hope Ever | 88 |
| Health is Wealth | 91 |
| Heavenly Wisdom | 92 |
| Human Beauty | 125 |
| Invocation to our Divinities | 102 |
| Invocation to the Infinite | 84 |
| Live Righteously | 99 |
| Life Builders | 103 |
| Life's Roses | 108 |
| Matter and Spirit | 100 |
| Nothing but Water to Drink | 89 |
| Our Country | 117 |
| On the Other Side | 119 |
| Over There | 120 |
| Prayer for the Virtues | 85 |
| Peace, Perfect Peace | 110 |
| Revelations of the Divine | 125 |
| Sun and Shadow | 87 |
| Spirit Hunger | 113 |
| The World is full of Beauty | 83 |
| The Inner Judge | 86 |
| The Religion of Health | 89 |
| The Senses | 90 |
| The Unity and Eternity of Labor | 92 |
| The Web of Life | 93 |
| True Womanhood | 95 |
| The Strength of the Faithful | 99 |
| The Kingdoms of Nature | 99 |
| The Three Rules | 101 |
| The True and the False | 101 |

## READINGS FOR FUNERALS.

| | PAGE |
|---|---|
| Song of the Silent Land | 174 |
| Farewells | 175 |
| Resignation | 175 |
| Life will attain its Completeness | 176 |
| Yielding up the Form | 177 |
| The Night is brief | 177 |
| Unfading Hope | 177 |
| Death hath made no Breach | 178 |
| Death of the Young | 178 |

| | PAGE |
|---|---|
| Banner Exercises | 171 |
| Banners and Badges | 144 |
| Badges | 148 |
| Constitution | 132 |
| Conversational Questions | 151 |
| Calisthenics | 156 |
| Celebrations | 169 |
| Funeral Services | 173 |
| General Subjects | 149 |
| Group Standards | 142 |
| Groups | 142 |
| Individual Development | 149 |
| Lyceum Anniversaries | 170 |
| Moral Lessons | 149 |
| Marching | 164 |
| Membership | 150 |
| Object Lessons | 154 |
| Physical Perfection | 156 |
| Pestalozzian Maxims | 148 |
| Philosophy and Language of Colors | 135 |
| Programme for a Lyceum Session | 167 |
| Promotions | 169 |
| Practical Suggestions | 180 |
| Parliamentary Rules | 181 |
| Scale of Colors, and their corresponding Groups | 141 |
| The Bell and Signals | 166 |
| The Golden Chain | 105 |
| The Spirit World | 179 |
| Wand Movements | 157 |

www.ingramcontent.com/pod-product-compliance
Lightning Source LLC
Chambersburg PA
CBHW020254170426
43202CB00008B/362